AF334520

George Sand
and the Victorian World

George Sand
and the Victorian World

PAUL G.
BLOUNT

ATHENS
The University of Georgia Press

Set in Linotype Sabon
Printed in the United States of America

Library of Congress Cataloging in Publication Data

Blount, Paul Groves.
George Sand and the Victorian world.
Bibliography.
Includes index.
1. Sand, George, pseud. of Mme. Dudevant, 1804–1876—Influence. 2. English literature—19th century—History and criticism. I. Title.
PQ2414.B5 843'.8 78-4274
ISBN 0-8203-0451-4

For my friend and mentor of old at Cornell University,
Francis E. Mineka,
and for my wife,
Mary Galloway Blount

Contents

Acknowledgments

My interest in George Sand began years ago at Westminster College, Fulton, Missouri, and at Cornell University, long before there was much interest in Sand's books or her life. I am grateful to many people who have assisted me in various stages of this work from handwritten copy through the index: Robert C. Gaissert was of great help; also Lex McMillan, Lee Vincent, and Elizabeth Kraft. I am indebted also to Brenda Azurmendi and to Brenda Coker for typing various editions of the manuscript. Librarians at Georgia State University, Emory University, Cornell University, and Carnegie Library in New York City were also most helpful.

Paul G. Blount

Georgia State University

I

George Sand, Fair and Foul

And all foul fiction is lèse majesté to the Madonna and to womanhood. . . .

George Sand is often immoral; but she is always beautiful.

John Ruskin, "Fiction Fair and Foul"

Warnings abound in every age against frivolous readings that may usher the reader over the threshold of sin. Francesca and Paolo in Dante's *Divine Comedy* were reading "of Lancelot, how love constrained him" before they committed the adultery that condemned them to hell. Three centuries later, in Sheridan's play *The Rivals,* Sir Anthony Absolute stated the case: "Madam, a circulating library in a town is an evergreen tree of diabolical knowledge! It blooms through the year! And depend upon it . . . that they who are so fond of handling the leaves, will long for the fruit at last" (I. ii. 235–39). Hannah More wrote in 1819 against the seductive powers of literature, especially French fiction, that led to a violation of marriage vows and contributed to divorce. She recommended the exclusion of all such works from family reading. French fiction had become associated so naturally with evil that a pharisaical monk in Browning's "Soliloquy of the Spanish Cloister" plots to send a fellow monk whom he hates to hell by tricking him into inadvertently looking at pages of a "scrofulous French novel. . . . Simply glance at it, you grovel / Hand in foot in Belial's gripe" (ll. 57, 59–60).

For thoughtful Victorians the problem of French fiction had many facets. First, the reading population in Britain in the nineteenth century had become wide based and was growing. In an age when the novel reached its peak of popularity, more fiction was published than ever before; by 1839 a new reading public was eagerly consuming serial publications of *Oliver Twist* and *Pickwick Papers,* and in 1847 the first installment of *Vanity Fair* appeared. By the end of the century Dickens, Thackeray, Eliot, Hardy, and the Brontës were secure in their fame. In addition a host of lesser figures tried their hand at fiction: to mention only a few, Edward Bulwer-Lytton, Mary Mitford, Charles Kingsley, Robert Louis Stevenson, Anthony Trollope, Thomas Hughes, Elizabeth Gaskell, Charles Reade, and Wilkie Collins. Political leaders like Disraeli and religious figures like Newman also wrote novels. To compound an already complicated problem, foreign books were being imported on a wide scale: for example, in 1835, using a population ratio, one French volume was imported for every fifty-three Englishmen.[1] In spite of this great demand there lurked a suspicion that the French could be guilty of greater excesses than the British and that the French were more innovative. Reinforcing their enduring fear of the seductive powers of literature, most Victorians were convinced that a great sexual dam was about to break, to inundate all of society, sweeping away the church, the family, and indeed the entire social structure. Uneasy as they often were about the structure, many Victorians feared even more what might replace it, particularly if the new order came from a French source.

On this troubled British scene appeared the numerous

works and the striking personality of Aurore Lucile Dupin, now famous under her masculine pen name of George Sand. Of all the colorful personalities that populated the nineteenth century, Sand often dominated, and her life, reported in detail to the Victorians, increased the fame of her works. Since her life and ancestry were of a kind with her controversial prose, she seemed to fulfill the old British adage "Blood will tell."

Born 1 July 1804 Aurore Lucile Dupin could, by various illegitimate connections, claim illustrious and infamous ancestors in a family where Maurice and Aurore were traditional given names. Sand's great-great-grandfather was the Elector of Saxony, who became King of Poland; he sired over three hundred bastards. The memoirs of Sand's great-great-grandmother, the Countess of Königsmark, caused a critic in the *Foreign Quarterly* to comment in 1836 that the Countess's times rivaled those of the Romans in corruption. A son born out of wedlock to the Elector and the Countess later became Comte de Saxe and a Marshal of France. He also sired a child out of wedlock, the second Aurore, who married an aging aristocrat. Their son Maurice, while serving in Napoleon's army in 1804, married a young camp follower, Sophie Delaborde, just in time to legitimatize their daughter Aurore, the future George Sand. After her father died young, the third Aurore spent her childhood with her loyalties divided between two women who hated each other, her mother and her paternal grandmother. The mother, a daughter of a Parisian birdseller, might well have found her way into a Balzac novel, while the grandmother was an aristocrat trained in the thought of the eighteenth-century philosophes. Because of her wealth, the grandmother won out as legal guardian. Sand spent many happy days at her grandmother's pleasant country estate at Nohant, which the old woman had bought to escape Paris at the time of the Revolution. Sand inherited the estate upon her grandmother's death. Partly to spite her mother, Sand made a very ill-advised marriage to Casimir Dudevant, the illegitimate but acknowledged son of a baron. Her husband little understood her, and to this unhappy marriage two children were born, Maurice and Solange.

Sand adored her son but misunderstood, and was misunderstood by, her daughter. As André Maurois writes in his biography of Sand, all of the women in Sand's family had sons and lovers and they loved their sons more than they loved their lovers.[2] One of Sand's lovers was Jules Sandeau, for whom she abandoned her family to live in Paris. In 1831, after collaborating with Sandeau, she published her first novel, *Indiana,* under the name of George Sand. It was a novel about unconventional love and the first of over sixty novels, most of them controversial, that she would write. For the next two decades she would seek happiness and self-fulfillment in love affairs with Prosper Merimée, Alfred de Musset, Dr. Pietro Pagello, Michel de Bourges, and Frédéric Chopin. By publicly adopting masculine dress and smoking cigars she became identified in the press as the first of the New Women. She gained additional notoriety by her active role in liberal French politics.

Popular notions in fact arose in Sand's day that she lived her books then wrote them. Franz Liszt, an old friend, made the observation that Sand treated her lovers like butterflies: first she captured them; then she preserved them in her novels.[3] Oscar Wilde commented that Sand, like Goethe, had first to live her loves before she could write about them; and the age was one, Wilde noted, when a broken heart might run to several editions.[4]

Sand's books were eagerly sought out in the nineteenth century, and a fascination with her ideas was not restricted to France alone, for other continental countries, England, and America responded to her. In Poland readers saw her as a champion of freedom, as did Italian patriots. In Germany her *Lélia* became the model for a popular kind of novel. Among the Russians, Dostoevski and Turgenev admitted an indebtedness; in America Whitman reflected her influence; Emerson and Henry James admired her.[5]

England was in ferment in many ways during the period from 1832 to 1876 when Sand was publishing, and she was a part of that ferment. References to her occur in the letters of Matthew Arnold, George Eliot, Jane Carlyle, Elizabeth Barrett Browning, Charlotte Brontë, and other literary figures; moreover, an examination of a dozen leading British periodicals of the period shows that Sand's works were frequently reviewed. Regardless of her popularity, Sand's life and works did not endear her to the English Puritan nor to the press that acted as guardian of his morality.

It is surprising that she was read so widely in an age much concerned about propriety, but there are a number of reasons why Victorians took her as seriously as they did. Sand's age recognized her for what she was, the first of the modern women: she became the symbol of the emancipated female at a time when the rights of women assumed a growing importance in the thinking of the Victorians. A country that produced Mary Wollstonecraft's *A Vindication of the Rights of Women* as early as 1797 and later, in 1869, John Stuart Mill's *On the Subjection of Women* could not ignore Sand's writings in which women's rights, particularly in matters of love, were fervently presented. To many Victorian women of independent mind, such as Charlotte Brontë, Jane Carlyle, Elizabeth Browning, and George Eliot, Sand became a compelling symbol, championing the rights of two of England's most depressed groups: women and the working class. Sand also became linked with the Saint-Simonians, associated in many British minds with ideas of free love and political revolution.

At a time when France seemed to many Europeans the arena in which the future destiny of Europe might be foreshadowed, Sand symbolized a major force in the political affairs of France. To the British Tory, frightened by the French Revolutions of 1789, 1830, and 1848, she was a female to be mistrusted and an author unfit to be read by respectable people. Yet liberals like George Eliot and Joseph Mazzini, an Italian revolutionary in exile in England, had great admiration for her. Because of her associations with French socialists Leroux and Lamennais and because of her socialist novels like *Le Meunier d'Angibault,* she was as often acclaimed for her ideas as she was admired for her literary worth.

Finally, Sand was appreciated as an important literary artist and drew praise from ordinary readers, the workaday critics, and the literati. Many who opposed her, as Ruskin did, nevertheless had to admit her power as an artist. Late in the nineteenth century, critic Leslie Stephen urged Thomas Hardy to imitate Sand's *Maîtres-Sonneurs*. In addition to appreciating her style, a great many Victorians perused her pages to find answers for troubled times, trusting her as a literary sage or prophet, turning to her as they once turned to their Bibles. Mazzini spoke of a "small number of chosen souls, the initiative and precursive of every country who commune with her from afar."[6] He commented how much some of Sand's early *Lettres d'un Voyageur* had meant to him when he was engaged in the politics of revolutionary Italy and troubled in his personal life. George Eliot described Sand as "one of the writers who have rolled away the waters from their bed, raised new mountains and spread delicious valleys for me."[7] An examination of Matthew Arnold's *Note-Books* shows that he turned frequently to Sand to find a criticism of the age and a hope for the future. She was one of the authors he read in formative years as he built his philosophy of literature as a *magister vitae,* a director of life.

It is not an exaggeration to say that a cult of George Sand existed in Victorian England and that among its participants were some of the most important figures in the literary world. Others were just as vociferous in their dislike of her. Literate Victorians found Sand fair or foul, to use Ruskin's phrase, but they could not ignore her.

Many read her in the original French. An examination of reviews written in the 1830s and 1840s by Mary Margaret Busk, John Wilson Croker, George Henry Lewes, Frances Trollope, William Thackeray, and Joseph Mazzini reveals that the reviewer usually quoted from the original French edition or rendered his own translation.

Writers like Elizabeth Barrett, Jane Carlyle, George Eliot, Matthew Arnold, Charlotte Brontë, and John Stuart Mill also read Sand in the original. General education and travel increased the ability of many Englishmen to handle the language, and if anyone needed help, private tutors abounded. For Englishmen who could not read French, translations appeared from time to time. By the end of the 1840s Englishmen could read in translation Sand's controversial religious novel *Spiridion,* her "innocent" *Mosaic Worker,* her *Consuelo* (which Matthew Arnold mentioned in his anniversary essay as her most popular work in England), the pastoral *Haunted Marsh* (*La Mare au Diable*), or one of her socialistic novels. *Indiana, Valentine,* and *Lélia,* all with sexual themes, have no translations listed this early in the *British Museum Catalogue* or the *English Catalogue of Books;* it is possible that these novels were too controversial for a publisher to risk a translation.

The Victorians read critical assessments of Sand's works in numerous periodicals that helped to mold British opinions during the period. All of them reflected some particular religious or political bias that resulted in either a favorable or unfavorable opinion of Sand. Matthew Arnold's demand for "disinterestedness" grew out of a national need for an unbiased publication, as even a casual examination of leading periodicals will demonstrate. A good illustration is the *Quarterly Review,* whose Tory position is reflected in drafts of articles supplied by conservatives like the Duke of Wellington, Sir Robert Peel, and Lord Stanley. The *Quarterly* opposed change and was hysterically faithful to British institutions, the church, the monarchy, and the landed aristocracy. Vitriolic John Wilson Croker, nemesis of the romantics, a harsh critic of Keats and Tennyson, apologized in the *Quarterly* for reviewing Sand, but he felt it necessary because "when we know, as we do know that they [French novels] find their way . . . into the hands of persons wholly or partially ignorant of their real character . . . we feel that it is our duty to stigmatize them with a BRAND which may awaken the attention of those who . . . unconsciously permit these conductors of moral contagion to infect their dwellings."[8]

The rival of the *Quarterly* in this period was the liberal *Edinburgh Review*. Yet the *Edinburgh,* tolerant of the novel as an art form and favorable in its reviews of French novels, merely praised Sand in passing and carried no review entirely devoted to her. Perhaps the *Edinburgh* did not see Sand's impact; or else it had no reason to fear her as did the *Quarterly*.

The Westminster Review, another Victorian periodical and an organ of the Benthamites, at first held the utilitarian view that fiction, being untrue, could mislead and impair judgment, but in 1836 John Stuart Mill, leader of the Utilitarians, merged his liberal *London Review* with the *Westminster*. Intense in his desire to dispel English insularity, Mill turned to the French and devoted much space to French literature; Sand's works met with favor in its pages.

Other periodicals such as the *Foreign Quarterly Review,* founded in 1827, kept English readers informed about current foreign literature. Mary Margaret Busk[9] and George Henry Lewes reviewed Sand in its pages. In 1865 the *Fortnightly Review* was founded by Anthony Trollope, James Cotter Morrison, and Frederick Chapman and modeled after the successful *Revue des Deux Mondes* (praised by Matthew Arnold as the kind of unbiased publication England did not have but needed). It was in the pages of the *Fortnightly* in 1877, a year after Sand's death, that Matthew Arnold published his appreciative essay on Sand. Weekly papers such as the *Athenaeum* and the *Saturday Review* also devoted space to literature and the arts. The *Athenaeum,* founded in 1828, had a foreign correspondent (probably Stendhal) who wrote a regular column "Literary Letter from Paris." Also in the pages of the *Athenaeum* Henry F. Chorley[10] looked upon the works of Sand with favor. The *Saturday Review,* on the other hand, was much more conservative; it disputed Arnold's claim of the superiority of the French masses over the British, condemned *Madame Bovary* on moral grounds, and opposed the emancipation of women. Yet by 1862 even the *Saturday Review* was full of praise for Sand and her novels.

These weeklies and quarterlies appealed to the better educated and to sophisticated opinion. The religious periodical, however, claimed a wider reading public. In 1828 the *Revue Encyclopédique* included fifty-nine such publications. Even though they did not review Sand they instilled negative attitudes in their readers. *The Methodist Magazine* and the *Baptist Magazine* sold for sixpence, and each had a circulation of over twenty thousand. Both distrusted French fiction. Read by a more intellectual audience were the magazines of the Unitarians, the *Monthly Repository* and the *Christian Reformer.* There were numerous other magazines for readers in the Church of England: the *Eclectic Review,* the *Christian Observer,* the

Quarterly Theological Review, and the *Christian Remembrancer* to name a few. All shades of established opinions were thus represented from conservative orthodoxy to evangelical enthusiasm. The Roman Catholic *Dublin Review* ignored Sand entirely, and her books were placed on the Index of Forbidden Books for Catholics in 1863. The influence of such periodicals on fiction was of course negative. Especially among the Evangelicals the moral principle was strongly applied in criticism. Moral judgments continued until the late sixties, when Evangelical reviews judged *A Tale of Two Cities* as "mere rubbish," *Jane Eyre* as a "free novel, heathen and horrid in taste," *Adam Bede* as vulgar, *Aurora Leigh* as "hysterically indecent," *Vanity Fair* as "morally disgusting," *Griffith Gaunt* as "immoral" ("the modesty and purity of woman cannot survive its perusal"), and the *Ordeal of Richard Feverel* as "indelicate."[11] Such opposition to fiction makes all the more interesting Sand's flourishing reputation. Yet in 1839 Mazzini wrote that Sand's novels were sold and read everywhere "not only in Piccadilly but we believe even in Albemarle Street." By 1847 Mazzini was able to boast in the *People's Journal:*

> But a few years ago and George Sand was, here in England, prejudged an *outlaw.* There was a terror in her name, a triple censure—religious, political, and social—upon her books. People took great care not to read them—they contented themselves with judging them. The few minds hardy enough to venture into the abyss were cautious not to avow it: They confessed to Paul de Kock and Balzac. From the height of its Gothic watchtower sounded the alarm-gun of the old *Quarterly.* Let the enemy but touch British ground with the sole of

his foot, and public morality was evidently ruined forever. The enemy has now penetrated to the very heart of the kingdom. George Sand is read, admired, and loved.[12]

Sand's champion, Mazzini, claimed that a conspiracy existed in the British press to ignore her, a silence he boasted that he had broken in 1839. It is true that Sand had published in 1832 and that her books were available; but except for scant notices in 1834 and 1835, Mazzini's was her first friendly review. In attempting to account for this phenomenon, Marcel Moraud, writing on the influence of French romanticism in England, states that French literature was favorably or unfavorably received in direct relation to the Englishman's attitude toward French politics; a survey of the periodicals of the day supports Moraud's contention.[13]

In addition to open hostility or conspiratorial silence from people who feared her, Sand's reputation had to contend with warnings to readers from her friends: Mary Margaret Busk, while generally laudatory in the *Foreign Quarterly,* warned that Sand was not for innocent young minds. Mazzini himself wrote that "spirits, young, pure, and innocent, not worn by unhappiness whom contact with the world has not yet endowed with the knowledge of evil" should abstain from reading Sand's works. George Henry Lewes, one of Sand's strongest champions, admitted that Sand held "some few opinions on religious, moral and political subjects, which are at variance with those generally received."

Sharpe's London Magazine printed an article by Julia Ward Howe in which the American author described an indebtedness she had felt in her youth to Sand's novels:

Did not all of us feel, in our young admiration for her, something of the world's great struggle between conservative discipline and revolutionary inspiration? We knew our parents would not have us read her, *if they knew*. We knew they were right. Yet we read her at stolen hours, with waning and still entreated light; and as we read, in a dreary, wintry room, with a flickering candle warning us of late hours and confiding expectations, the atmosphere grew warm and glorious about us, a true human company, a living sympathy crept near us, the very world seemed not the same world after as before. She had given us a real gift; no criticism could take it away. The hands might be sinful, but the box they broke contained an exceeding precious ointment.[14]

But now a parent herself, the critic saw Sand's novels in a different light: "Grown mothers ourselves, we quietly remove them as far as possible from the young hands about us, and would rather have deprived them of the noble French language altogether than have allowed it to bring them such lessons as Jacques and Valentine."

Much as she admired Sand, Elizabeth Barrett could not read all of her works: " 'Leila' again, made me blush in my solitude to the ends of my fingers—flush three blushes in one—for her who could be so shameless—for her sex, whose purity she so disgraced—and for myself in particular who could hold such a book for five minutes in one hand while a coal-fire burnt within reach of the other."[15]

Regardless of why Englishmen read Sand, she seems to have been read more widely in England than any other foreign writer except Goethe.[16] But whether the English perceived her as a prototype of the emancipated woman, as political symbol or as literary genius, the moral issue dominated the criticism of her works through the 1860s.

Many critics attacked her private life to discredit her literary productions, using the axiom enunciated in the early writings of John Ruskin that great art is the product of a right-minded artist on the one hand and a pure and vigorous society on the other. An intellectual, emancipated female who left her husband and who openly paraded her amours was hardly a "right-minded artist." Nor were her novels in which situations abound like the one in *Jacques* where the husband commits suicide so that his wife can join her lover likely to build a pure and vigorous society. Even though many of Sand's friends, like George Henry Lewes and Joseph Mazzini, defended her works, the moral issue continued to rage and was intensified because she was a woman with intellectual pretensions.

II

Sand, Victorian Antifeminism, and the Tradition of the Fig Leaf

> Dr. Livingstone says of some of the African tribes, that "they seem to have lost all tradition of the fig leaf."
>
> T. C. Sandars

Writing about George Sand in the Unitarian *National Review* in 1858, Oxonian T. C. Sandars cogently observed that to all the difficulties implied in the fact that Sand was a *French* writer of contemporary fiction was added the difficulty that "she is a woman, and what is more a woman with a philosophical turn of mind."[1] For Victorians there was also the issue of the plainness of Sand's language, which Sandars called too indelicate for use in ordinary conversation. He then recalled Dr. Livingstone's comment about uncivilized, naked Africans and quoted Livingstone on the tradition of the fig leaf, implying the necessity of the tradition if civilization were to survive. The question of whether Sand was an enemy or a friend of civilization dominated Victorian criticism much more than the literary value of her works. Much Victorian fascination for Sand or detestation of her stemmed from the fact that she was the first of the modern emancipated women.

J. W. Croker, already disturbed by the "union of impassioned rhetoric and sensual ideas" that he found in Victorian novels, was further disturbed when he discovered that Sand's "lascivious tales" were the product of "a lady with a title," and Croker quoted Edward Young: "A shameless woman is the worst of men."[2] It was customary for reviewers in this period to apologize when they were being hostile to women. Croker made a bow to the custom; yet he displayed no chivalric forbearance for the gentler sex when he dealt with Sand: in an understatement he insisted he would show Madame Sand no deference in his reviews; her adopting a masculine name removed any protection she might claim as a woman. This same feeling that Sand had desexed herself appears when Patrick Kennedy, an assistant in Kildare Place School, Dublin, described Sand as "an accomplished Amazon, proficient, as a young girl, in botany but scarcely able to repeat the Lord's prayer." As a mature adult she poured her energies into works "upholding unholy love" and in shocking language not fit for use in mixed company made "determined assaults on the bulwarks of social order and family happiness."[3] An unidentified critic in Bentley's *Quarterly Review,* commenting on Sand's *Histoire de ma Vie,* complained, "the sirens did not print their enchantments nor write their lives."[4]

Yet there were contrasting opinions: Joseph Mazzini, a strong supporter of women's emancipation, reveled in the fact of Sand's femininity. He was confident no man could have written *Lettres d'un Voyageur* and when he was sure of her identity exclaimed: "Thanks be to God, Sand is a woman."[5] Some women writers, however, were reluctant to recognize Sand as a sister. Mary Margaret Busk generally praised Sand in her reviews but admitted that she was amazed when she first discovered Sand was a woman;

she was pleased to report she had been informed (but could not vouch) that Sand was of unblemished character. Mrs. Busk did not praise all of Sand's "daring situations" and "graphic delineations," however, for she questioned the propriety of Sand's works for youthful readers.[6] While the emancipated Frances Trollope praised Sand's genius, calling her an "ornament of the age," she also felt that Sand's volumes should be closed to the "young and the innocent," and she would not "dare to name her among those to whom the memory clings with gratitude as the giver of high mental enjoyment."[7]

William Thackeray, who chided Mrs. Trollope for going to France and writing mainly about tea parties, was fascinated with Sand's works but revealed his Anglo-Saxon prudery when he complained that a Frenchman would think no more of boasting that he had a mistress than that he had a tailor, while in England such action adopted the "decency of secrecy." Thackeray found Sand's *Indiana* an attack on marriage, and while he thought French marriage laws "pressed cruelly upon unfortunate women," he doubted Sand to be the judge of such matters any more than one would go to a pickpocket to ask if the "stealing of pocket-handkerchiefs or snuff-boxes may or may not be vicious."[8]

Thackeray's comment about the decency of secrecy is at the heart of the matter; Sand's first novels, *Valentine* and *Indiana,* do not depict relations between the sexes any differently from what they were in Victorian England, and the theme of seduction is not uncommon in Victorian fiction. But the fact that such situations are openly discussed from a woman's point of view was more than many Victorian critics could abide. W. R. Greg's comment about Sand's *Elle et Lui* (based on Sand's liaison with Musset) is to this point: "Nothing," Greg wrote, "can be more disgraceful than the things revealed . . . except the revelation of them."[9]

Much of the admiration for Sand, or fear of her, was linked to ideas Englishmen had about the Saint-Simonian movement, which started in France about the time of the publication of Sand's first novels. *Indiana* appeared in 1832, at the same time Saint-Simonian missionaries arrived in England preaching a new Utopia based upon the teachings of their founder, Comte de Saint-Simon, who advocated abolition of the military system, abolition of the right to inherit property, an end to competition in business and industry, better pay for the working class, and women's rights. On the last point Saint-Simonians argued that through institutionalized Christianity society had imposed laws that forbade polygamy yet still granted men the right of "scortatory love" while it denounced women who parted from a strict line of conduct.[10] Of all the issues in the Saint-Simonian program their arguments for sexual freedom had the most powerful impact on the English. To many conservatives Saint-Simonian teachings in Sand's writings advocated free love and foreshadowed a complete breakdown of the family structure.

For a short time the Saint-Simonians appealed to intellectuals in France and England who wanted change and especially to two of England's most oppressed groups: the working class and women. The Saint-Simonians preached what they considered to be a new kind of Christianity that blended mysticism and rationalism. Furthermore their leaders in France were young men of ability, often aristocrats, who were willing to act to bring about their vision of a better future. Comte de Saint-Simon himself had served in America under Lafayette. The group attracted the attention in England of John Stuart Mill, who was sympathetic to the movement but never became an open advocate. Saint-Simonians also corresponded with Carlyle, and one of their leaders, Gustave d'Echthal, called on Carlyle before the group began its missionary drive to convert England, a drive that had very limited success. Because the Saint-Simonians attacked the status quo in three areas sacred to conservatives—property, home, and church—conservatives vilified the Saint-Simonians in the press. They were charged with being intent on instructing females in the art of prostitution. Robert Southey attacked Saint-Simonian reforms in the pages of the Tory *Quarterly Review*. Tennyson prayerfully wrote that surely "hearts as true and pure as steel in old England" would "never brook the sight of Baal in the sanctuary, and Saint-Simon in the Church of Christ."[11] Englishmen easily linked Sand with the Saint-Simonians because her first works, *Indiana, Valentine,* and *Lélia,* dealt with marriage as an institution that had failed. It is probable that many Englishmen who had not heard of Robert Owen, Charles Fourier, or Saint-Simon knew of their ideas on marriage through Sand's novels.

Two of Sand's biographers, André Maurois and Vladimir Karenine, think that Sand was influenced less by the Saint-Simonian movement than by her lover Pierre Leroux and the Abbé de Lamennais. Both men were propagandists with theories of social equality whose ideas were close to those of the Saint-Simonians. Holding a faith in human perfectibility, they believed that humanity could save itself through love and the proper use of the arts and science.

But the question of influence is academic. These revolutionary ideas were current; Sand embraced them and became for many Victorians the prototype of a revolutionist advocating change, especially in women's rights. Even the Saint-Simonians recognized the affinity: Sand was offered the title of *Mère* by a Saint-Simonian politician and journalist. In this role she would have been the female counterpart of Barthélemy Prosper Enfantin, the *Père* or "Supreme Father" of all the Saint-Simonians. Sand recognized points of agreement but gently declined the honor. If Saint-Simonians felt Sand to be the female messiah, destined to pronounce on women's rights, it is little wonder that Englishmen regarded her in the same light.

In the preface of a later edition of *Indiana,* Sand replied to the charge of Saint-Simonian sympathies: "At the time I wrote *Indiana,* the cry of Saint-Simonism was raised on every pretext." After protesting her innocence, she added, "Even were he [the author] more mature and more skillful, he would not dare to lay his hand upon the great sores of a dying civilization." One of those "great sores" was the institution of marriage. And in the minds of many Victorians Sand did lay her hand upon it.

The best example of Victorian morality intruding upon literary criticism is found in reviews by John Wilson Croker in the *Quarterly Review.* Croker wrote because he felt morally obligated to warn the public: young ladies were reading French novels and a female book club of "antick character" had recently been duped into buying Balzac's novels. To prevent the misuse of French novels by the innocent, Croker wished to label them as apothecaries label poison. He believed all contemporary French novels were dangerous, having their origins in the writings of Jean Jacques Rousseau, whom Croker characterized as a "liar, cheat, and thief, who had no morals whatever." He cited Rousseau's *Héloïse* as a model for Sand's novels, all based on "an ill-assorted marriage and an adulterous amour." Croker said he could not see, after reading *Indiana,* that Sand had any love of virtue:

> The story is not fuller of wickedness than of absurdities, and the *dénouement* is quite in character. Indiana, having lost her husband by death and her lover by infidelity, resolves to commit suicide; but is persuaded by a stupid cousin, who accompanies her throughout the novel with a *brotherly* attachment, not to do it in Europe, but to go all the way to the Isle of France in the East Indian seas, where the act may be romantically executed by tumbling down a certain precipice, with which, in the days of their infancy, these two cousins, both natives of that island, had been acquainted; they sail for the Isle of France—they arrive—they take a considerable time to refresh themselves after their long voyage, and to prepare themselves for a longer one. At last one night, when all is ready, they retire to the mountains, they approach the precipice—they contemplate from the cliff the boiling torrent into which they are to throw themselves—they find it in all respects an exceptionably convenient place for their purpose—they take a last embrace—advance hand in hand to the edge of the precipice—pause for a moment to admire the moon—sit down to wait till a cloud shall come to veil their fatal deed in congenial obscurity—but they tarry rather too long, and begin to hesitate.
>
> Next morning finds them still alive, seated on the rock; and

the next evening finds them—more comfortably, but less romantically—*in bed together,* without any interference of either priests or magistrate.

Croker submits *Valentine* to the same moralistic ridicule:

M. LeComte de Raimbault has two daughters, Louise and Valentine—Louise, poor lady, has had a—misfortune! for which her father—instigated by her stepmother—not only turns her out of doors, but shoots the seducer through the head—a vengeance which the author makes still more natural by informing us that the deceased was the gallant not only of the daughter, but of the wife of the count.[12]

To the modern reader *Indiana* and *Valentine* are interesting as period pieces, quite dated, and not at all shocking in theme or language. The young female Werther for whom the latter book is named is too long-suffering and struggles against such odds that final yielding to illicit love makes her seem more a victim of fate than an advocate of free love. She finally yields to Benedict, who has fought against his passion with a valor equal to Valentine's, only after she has been abandoned by her grandmother, sister, mother, and husband, all of whom she has appealed to for help. In the end sin is punished, ironically just when the two could have become legally man and wife. The novel must have pleased Sand's readers seeking vicarious experience, for an expectation of seduction is maintained for two hundred pages, but the shock value lay in Sand's own personal reputation as a woman championing free love in, what was then, very frank language.

Croker gave to *Jacques* only one paragraph of biting satire in spite of the fact that it is the story of a wife's affair and the husband's noble sacrifice of himself so the wife and lover can be happy together. It is Sand's *Lélia* that Croker found so revolting that the best he could do was select five quotations, which he gave judiciously in the original French. The first illustration quotes a monk who in declaring his guilty love for Lélia utters her name in the same breath with the Virgin Mary. Another quotation states that according to the plan of providence the union of man and woman should be temporary. In the third excerpt Pulchérie (Lélia's sister and her foil) urges Lélia to become a courtesan since she cannot become a nun. Another passage praises suicide as a refuge against man and offers nihilism as a refuge against God; and the last quotation praises the "virginal soul" of a prostitute.

Croker assured his readers that these were commonplace compared with passages that swarm throughout *Lélia* and then did what was commonplace in Victorian criticism. He focused on the moral influence, applying the fiction as a "director of life," influencing society rather than merely commenting upon it.

Quoting French newspapers for his evidence, he found an increase in suicide, listing 110 between September and December; the suicides were often by young people who loved in spite of conventional morality and parental objection. Four pages of Croker's review provided details: one halfhearted attempt at suicide by a lover who had killed his mistress (another man's wife); a murder, which Croker attributes to an illicit affair Sand describes in *Valentine;* the murder of an illegitimate child by a mother who had killed seven other children (when police searched her house, they found "seven corpses of children, smoked and dried"); the murder of a son by an angry father. This last situation Croker compared to Sand's *André,* and he asked, "Who can tell whether that fiction may not have tended to produce in the mind of the young man the obstinacy which exasperated the unnatural atrocity." Croker feared that this "flood of impurity" in French life might carry the French back to the horrors and depravity of post-Revolution days. As an example Croker referred to dramatic exhibitions during the "first Revolution," *Herbert and Gobel, Goddess of Reason,* and *Spectacle de la Nature,* "which the reader . . . cannot imagine the depravity . . . the actors and actresses were at no expense for a wardrobe."[13]

In the 1840s England had not developed the level of criticism which Carlyle or Arnold demanded and more nearly got by the 1870s. Frances Trollope tried, and her reviews revealed an urbanity lacking in Croker, for her feminism made her separate George Sand the writer from Aurore Dupin the woman. Still, like Croker, she saw literature influencing the times adversely and admitted that some of Sand should be "closed to the young and innocent," but (like Arnold thirty years later) she praised Sand's love of nature and her philosophy of love and hope. She recommended *André* and *Mattea.* There is evidence in her biography that Mrs. Trollope tried to learn little about Sand's private life, saying that such knowledge should not affect criticism.[14]

William Makepeace Thackeray allied himself with Croker's chauvinistic, puritanical view. He chided French frankness, particularly when dealing with relations between the sexes. In an article entitled "Madame Sand and the New Apocalypse," Thackeray characterized *Indiana* as an "eloquent attack on marriage, told in a parable running to two volumes." Of *Valentine* he complained that Sand gave young men and women "the same tender license." *Lélia* he found to be a "topsyturvyfication of morality, a thieves' and prostitutes' apotheosis."[15] Yet in spite of the adverse commentary a close reading reveals that Thackeray was fascinated with Sand.

An unidentified critic in an 1841 *Athenaeum* review displays a typical Victorian balance. His review reveals a fascination with Sand—like Mrs. Trollope and Arnold, he admired her nature descriptions—yet the review, which deals with *A Winter in the South of Europe* (Sand's account of her stay at Majorca with Chopin), does not mention Chopin by name but refers to him only as "an accomplished musician in Sand's group" and sidesteps comments which he said reflected doctrines of Lamennais and his sect. The critic chastises Sand for "a morbid vitality, a perverted eloquence, with which the English have little sympathy." He finds in her works a general bitterness of tone that "proclaims a mind ill at ease with itself, and an . . . intolerance which flourishes nowhere more rankly than in those who confound loose opinion suiting loose practice with universal toleration."[16]

From the late 1830s throughout the 1840s, Sand's views on freedom between the sexes and the explicitness of her language set the attitudes of Victorian critics toward her and her works. A *Foreign Quarterly* reviewer in 1838 identified Sand as "a lady who wrote novels which most men would blush to write";[17] a writer in the *Foreign Quarterly Review* in 1841 identified her further as the most dangerous of all writers guilty of "advocating the absolute emancipation of woman from all moral and social obligations, and the destruction of the marriage tie." He alerted his readers to the contagion that would spread from her novels that advocated trial marriages, a contagion that eventually might not allow the institution of marriage to exist at all:

> The self-styled emancipators of woman, the asserters of her rights, whether male or female, will accomplish nothing beyond reducing that beautiful creation of maiden, wife, and mother to a mere impure being. The French novels of the present day are but narrations of the metamorphosis of woman into the vile type; representing, as it were, a second fall of Eve from testing a new fruit of knowledge. Warnings and animadversions on these French doctrines are the more called for at present, inasmuch as the contagion has already begun to spread amongst ourselves.[18]

Although he makes no direct reference to Sand, a writer in the liberal *Edinburgh Review* admitted in 1843 that there were few French novels that Englishmen would translate literally. An 1848 reviewer in *Blackwood's* called Sand a "great favorite" but confessed that her earlier novels had earned her the title "Muse of Adultery."[19]

The most vitriolic review, aside from Croker's, was one by a writer in the conservative *Foreign and Colonial Quarterly Review*. After congratulating his reading audience that Providence had not willed England's fate to be the same as France's, with each Englishman engaging in extreme individualism or in "swine-like animalism," he wrote not literary indictments of Sand but indictments of her views on marriage and her advocacy of lying, adultery, and suicide. He criticized her masculine name, "hermaphrodite" dress, and use of tobacco:

> Having thus named and surnamed herself, she further thought fit to assume the privilege of having and wearing certain articles more unmistakeably and peculiarly masculine still . . . George Sand stood forth among the now at least, somewhat startled Parisian world, one of the stronger sex, in attire as well as name. . . . Still further to support her manly character with propriety, she is said to have addicted herself to a large and habitual consumption of tobacco.[20]

She would, he warned his English readers, reduce France to the "level of the ourang outang."

Religious periodicals, never primarily interested in belles lettres, were more provincial than the magazines mentioned above. If they looked at literature at all, it was certain to be English more often than French. Yet Sand's reputation was too great for the religious periodicals to overlook her entirely.

An 1840 critic in the *Eclectic Review,* a magazine of the Dissenters, warned readers to expect no morality from Sand's works. Gustave Masson in three numbers of *Wesley Methodist Magazine* in 1847 discussed French fiction, admitting that Sand headed the list of French writers who had broken the bonds of French neoclassicism; yet Masson criticized Sand chiefly for her views on sex. Her new absolution, he said, was "Her sins, which are many, are forgiven, for she loved much." Masson's religious bias dominated the article; he concluded by praying for a conversion that would save France from socialism, communism, Fourierism, neo-Christianity, atheism, and Romanism.[21]

The Evangelical *North British Review* in 1847 criticized Sand for her views on love, religion, and marriage and found fault with her revolutionary political views. In this periodical one reviewer criticized Sand's use of her own life as the subject of novels; of *Elle et Lui* (Sand's account of her affair with Musset), the reviewer commented: "how revolting was the bad taste which could induce a woman to dissect . . . her old lover . . . under the disguise of a most transparent art."[22]

An interesting anomaly in early Victorian criticism is found in an article that appeared in the *London and Westminster Review* in 1837. The reviewer calls it ridiculous to judge a nation by its fiction as Croker had done. He asks how typical of Scottish nobility is a situation in Sir Walter Scott's *St. Ronan's Well* in which a nobleman robs his elder son of his mistress and his birthright, then attempts to kill him. He considers another situation in *Adam Blair* in which a minister yields to a beautiful woman and asks how typical of Presbyterians? Or Catherine Gore's novels about frivolous women—how are they typical of England's fairer sex? Further he asks, can we judge Elizabethan morals by the plays of Massinger and Ford? The reviewer replies to his own questions with this statement: "The *Quarterly Review,* as everyone knows, is not famous for the strict honesty of its criticisms."[23]

Among all the adverse criticism Sand had two staunch defenders—the Italian patriot Joseph Mazzini and George Eliot's common-law husband, George Henry Lewes. Mazzini, who earned money for his support by reviewing literature while he was in exile in England, agreed with Sand politically. He argued early in the century, in 1839, that an author should be judged by his ability to satisfy the wants of his age. Also it is not enough, he wrote in another criticism of Sand in that same year, to say "Do not read," but one should say "Read in such a manner." He argued that adultery is not a common theme in Sand's books and that *Lélia* is in a class with *Faust* or *Manfred,* not for the innocent; the aim is good but details are horrible. Sand, he maintained, mirrored the times; she was like Rousseau, whose books might be banned but would return later in the French constitution. He praised Sand as a prophet of the future, like Homer, Dante, and Goethe. Mazzini further argued that a writer may be not entirely moral in all of his actions yet be capable of inspiring his readers to higher goals.[24] Mazzini continued to write on Sand over a six-year period, sometimes anonymously, sometimes under his own signature. His judgments were ultimately sound; he argued that one cannot lift a specific passage from a book and call the book obscene—an insight that would parallel United States Federal Judge van Pelt Bryan's 1959 decision on *Lady Chatterly's Lover.*

Entering the scene in 1840 was George Henry Lewes, whom Charles Eliot Norton characterized as having "the vanity of a Frenchman and not many more morals."[25] Lewes knew the Mazzini articles on Sand, liked them, and agreed with them. Just as Mazzini may have argued from a political bias, Lewes may be accused of a personal bias: he was unable to divorce a wife who had committed adultery because, in the eyes of the courts, he himself was a "bohemian." He praised Sand early in 1844 in the pages of the *Foreign Quarterly Review,* a periodical that approached literature from the "disinterested view" that Matthew Arnold urged twenty years later in his "Function of Criticism at the Present Time." His first article in 1844 considered Sand and Balzac from various points of view: as moralists, artists, and as entertainers. Sand emerged superior in all three categories and nowhere more superior than in the moral sphere. Finding all novelists, whether French, German or English, somewhat immoral, Lewes distinguished between writers who err out of tampering with morbid thoughts and those who err out of "erroneous convictions." Sand is of the former; Balzac and Eugene Sue are of the latter. Sand, Lewes maintained, is a moral writer who never opposed marriage but only its abuse; and only three of twenty-three novels deal with marriage and one of them from the husband's point of view. Lewes reminded readers that while adultery was a favorite theme of Victorian novelists, Sand's heroines fought to preserve their chastity. Like Shelley and Byron, Sand was strong food for strong minds and could be an undesirable influence on anyone who tended toward unsocial acts. Her books like *Lélia* were to be avoided by the young, the inexperienced, and perhaps by all females. Yet Sand's reputation for immorality had grown so that readers attempted to find something wrong, even in works as innocent as *Sept Cordes de la Lyre*. Lewes commented:

> Never was there a more notable instance of giving a dog a bad name and hanging him. Madame Sand has been known to travel in an androgynous costume; smokes cigars, is separated from her husband, and has been the theme of prolific scandal. The conclusion drawn was, that from such a person nothing but anti-social works could possibly be expected. The idea having once taken possession of men's minds, no subsequent examination could uproot it. The errors that have ensued are incalculable.[26]

As for the Saint-Simonian taint, Lewes's view was that Sand's ideas on female emancipation argued for "equal but not the same" and he quoted a long passage from *Lettres à Marcie* to prove his point. Sand was dangerous only in that she raised questions about problems to which there seemed to be no answers. If Lewes was right, this made Sand even more of an anathema to the Victorians, who were sure there were answers. To make his point Lewes misquoted from Tennyson's "Ulysses" without identifying poem or poet: "All experiences were an arch, where through gleams that untravelled worlds, *whose margin fades* forever and forever when we move." Comparing Sand and Balzac as artists, Lewes still applied ethical criteria: Sand was a greater artist than Balzac since she was true to life. She was also greater than many English writers whom mothers allowed daughters to read in spite of the fact that these novelists gave an untrue exaggerated view of life which made their women readers sentimental.[27] Twelve years later Lewes encouraged George Eliot to write an article for the *Westminster Review*, "Silly Novels by Lady Novelists," which expressed distaste for the unreal, sentimental novels of the day.[28]

Lewes attacked unfair criticism which had an adverse effect on an author's works, identifying Croker and the *Quarterly* article as an example. He cited innocent young ladies who had read Sand yet who had never discovered any immorality until they received the prejudiced view that French novels were synonymous with all that was horrible and blasphemous. He found particularly unprofessional criticism in which the commonplace practice was to quote from Sand's characters and attribute those sentiments to Sand. One might as well quote from Iago, John, Edmund, or Richard to prove Shakespeare's immorality.

Another review by Lewes, published two years later in the *Foreign Quarterly,* accused Sand of writing second-rate fiction about noncontroversial subjects. There was less passion in works such as *Jeanne, La Comtesse de Rudolstadt, Teverino, Le Meunier,* and *M. Antoine.* Lewes declared that by writing of noncontroversial subjects Sand had prostituted her talent and become less of an artist:

> How very pale are the colours in which George Sand now paints the passions she once depicted with such unrivalled energy and truth. The impassioned author of *Indiana, Jacques, Valentine,* and *Mauprat* is scarcely to be recognized in *La Comtesse de Rudolstadt, Jeanne, Teverino, Le Meunier* and *M. Antoine.* The fire that glowed with such energy is exhausted. Timid readers are no longer startled by the vehement impetuosity and daring truth with which the human heart laid bare; it beats feebly now; and if the timid be not startled, neither are they led away by irresistible fascination. Many worthy people will applaud the change; it makes the works more *moral,* as they say. We cannot but deplore it, for it makes the works commonplace. We cannot forget that the author was once a great poet, uttering in harmonious language the deep experience. It is a sad fall this poet makes when dropping into the conventional agonies and unreal passions of the circulating library.[29]

This passage is the essence of Lewes's and Mazzini's criticism; their thesis was that a work may remain moral even though it describes an immoral situation; on the contrary, a book that might not offend puritan tastes could give an unreal picture of life. A mark of Lewes's modernity as a critic is that as early as 1840 he championed the right of a woman artist to depict passion. Another minor point here contributes an insight to Lewes's sensitivity as a critic: he criticizes Sand's *Jeanne* because he found it to be the picture of a chaste woman who remained chaste not because she triumphed over passion but because she could not experience it. What Lewes probably did not know was that Saint-Beuve had had the same kind of insight into Sand's first edition of *Lélia*. Sand saw the aptness of the criticism and was fearful that the book would be read autobiographically, as indeed it was throughout Europe, where readers, accustomed to Byron, readily identified the hero of a work of fiction with the author. Sand rewrote *Lélia*, and in the new version the heroine turned her back on love out of social consciousness.

Lewes's liberal views were maintained in 1858 by T. C. Sandars in the *National Review*. Sandars argued that English readers considered Sand immoral only if English standards were involved. As a French writer Sand might well delineate situations of which French criticism approved. Thus Sandars enlarges upon Mazzini and Lewes in arguing that a novelist may write about an immoral situation yet remain moral. As evidence he quotes her attitude about loss of chastity: "Sand feels truly and deeply the mournfulness and the pity of the termination of purity." Sandars has sympathy for another romantic view: the importance of love as a means of self-fulfillment. He quite rightly sees the importance of love in Sand's works; it is a major theme, the staple of all her novels, and love is weighed for its effect on the individual with little thought of society. Love becomes a necessary part of human growth; as such, nothing can be denied in its name; love becomes a kind of religion. Sandars goes further in accepting this liberal view, adding the dictum: once love has ended, the tie ceases.[30]

A critic writing in the usually conservative *Saturday Review* shows how by 1862 this view had taken hold. Only in France, the critic wrote, could one turn to fiction as Sand had done in *Lélia* to shriek against God and the universe, and English readers had to understand this fact if they were to understand French fiction. After commenting on the amazement of English readers with Sand's "strange union of poetry and elevation with wild morality," the critic wrote satirically of the British method:

> In England we manage things differently. We do not want to have people pouring out their crude philosophy, or sounding the abyss of doubt, or calling God to the tiny bar of their babyish insolence. We think them silly or wicked . . . and kick them and keep them under if they defy our prohibition. This saves us from much nonsense and keeps up a general atmosphere of respectability. We are probably right, and society gains, on the whole, when it insists that everyone shall either walk in the beaten paths, or else hold their tongue.[31]

But not all Englishmen willingly submit; hence the justification for vicarious experience through French books like *Lélia*.

A similarly sympathetic review of Sand and women's rights appeared in 1872 in a periodical that labeled itself "An Illustrated Magazine of Light and Amusing Literature for the Hours of Relaxation, Richly Illustrated." The article treats Sand like the tempest-tossed heroine of a bad Victorian novel, more sinned against than sinning. The article speaks of Sand's universal acceptance in Russia, Italy, and England, where she had been recognized in "a magnificent sonnet by one of our greatest poetesses," a reference to Elizabeth Barrett Browning. The reviewer blamed French marriage customs for Sand's "excesses" in Paris with Jules Sandeau and commented on the naturalness of Sand's acceptance by a "number of women, suddenly finding a fiery interpreter of their smouldering sentiments of injury."[32] The review, probably written by a woman, was carried in a leap year issue that featured Amazons, ancient and contemporary, who had been victorious over male companions.

A fervid moralistic hostility to Sand extended into the 1870s and 1880s. Mrs. O. W. Oliphant as late as 1876 expressed disgust with Sand's version of her love affair with Alfred de Musset in *Elle et Lui* (and disgust with *Elle,* Paul de Musset's version of his brother's love affair with Sand, and disgust with the account rendered by Alfred de Musset's mistress, Louise Colet, in her *Lui*). A. Innes Shand, writing also in *Blackwood's* a year later, recommended that *Jacques* be "relegated to the *index expurgatorious*" because of its "ingenious perversion of all our old-fashioned moral notions." There were passages in the novel on the "physiology of the married state" which, were he to quote, he would be compelled to quote in the original French.[33]

Thus the frankness of her language remained an issue to the end of the 1880s. By 1877 the *London Quarterly Review,* a publication of the Methodists, doubted Saint-Simonian influences in the novels but criticized Sand for not setting an example in the very area in which women should exercise a beneficial influence, in domestic duties. Leslie Stephen wrote Thomas Hardy in 1867 that French writers like Sand and Balzac were less cramped in their treatment of sex than were English writers, Thackeray in particular; Stephen confessed his liking for Sand and Balzac yet agreed that "commonplace criticism is correct . . . as a rule they are prurient and indecent." Writing to C. E. Norton, Stephen admitted reading a great deal of Sand, "one of those precocious infants, whom I rather hate for obvious reasons."[34]

John Ruskin admired Sand's literary style but disliked the "moral aspect" of her writings. He predicted that Sand's and Victor Hugo's novels could not endure because they were "tainted." To Ruskin a novel could not be immoral and good. He disliked Sand's "taint and leprosy of animal passion idealised as a governing power of humanity . . . as the chief element of interest in the conduct of its histories." Using his own criterion that combined morality and aesthetics, Ruskin declared *The Vicar of Wakefield* as the world's best novel.[35]

Writing in the *Nineteenth Century,* Frederic W. H. Myers summarized the difficulty: Sand was a woman but the intellectual superior of most men. "A feminine Goethe," Myers wrote, "is more than mankind can endure."[36]

III

The Peaceful Temples of Innocence

> Her works . . . set the world on fire lighting men in prison where no cheer ever entered. But at the same time their pernicious flames consumed the peaceful temples of innocence.
> Heine

Sand's reputation as a "female Goethe" created about her an aura of grandeur for independent Victorian women like Elizabeth Barrett Browning, George Eliot, Charlotte Brontë, Jane Carlyle, and her friend Geraldine Jewsbury, who while recognizing Sand's seductive powers insisted upon her greatness. Before Browning called on Elizabeth Barrett at Wimpole Street, she wrote:

> The dangerous point in George Sand appears to me to lie in the irresistible power she attributes to human passion. The *moral* of "Jacques" . . . to apply such a term to the most immoral of lessons, . . . is just that Love, . . . guilty love, observe, . . . cannot be resisted by the strongest will and most virtuous individuality. Then the disgusting tendency she has towards representing the passion of love under its physical aspect. I could not read Leilia for all its eloquence . . . however she is great, and capable of noble elevations both intellectual and moral: and I should not be ashamed before the whole world, to confess my sense of this.[1]

At the same time the future Mrs. Browning wrote her friend Henry F. Chorley, the critic, who also admired Sand, to state her envy of Sand's independence:

> I am more of a latitudinarian in literature than is generally thought expedient for women to be; and I have that admiration for genius which dear Mr. Kenyon calls my "immoral sympathy with power;" and if Madame Dudevant is not the first female genius of any country or age, I really do not know who is. And then she has certain nobleness—granting all the evil and "perilous stuff"—nobleness and royalness which makes me loyal.

After she had escaped her father's tyranny, Elizabeth expanded on her obligation to Sand:

> Do you know how much I love France and the French? Robert laughs at me for the mania of it. . . . When I was a prisoner, my other mania for imaginative literature used to be administered to me through the prison bars by Balzac, George Sand, and like immortal proprieties. They kept the colour in my life to some degree and did good service in their time to me, I can assure you, though in dear discreet England one oughtn't to confess to such reading, I believe, or you told me so yourself one day.[2]

George Eliot was less extravagant in her praise of Sand, but her calmer expression is only a matter of difference in personality. She found Sand's *Jacques* not shocking but "quite preternaturally true" in the description of the "psychological anatomy of . . . the early days of their marriage" and termed their story "an everyday tragedy."[3] Marcel Moraud states that Eliot turned to Sand for "intellectual food, which was able to a certain point to replace the religion she had renounced."[4] The account of her father's reaction when Eliot first confessed she could not accompany him to chapel because she had lost her faith supports Moraud's contention. Her father told her to throw out French novels, "all that rigmarole you're always pouring over. I always knew those frog-eaters couldn't put anything but nonsense in your head."[5] Moraud thinks Eliot would not have become the common-law wife of George Henry Lewes without the influence of Sand. Certainly it was Lewes and Sand who changed Mary Ann Evans into George Eliot. The fact that she took George as part of her pen name is significant, since it was also Sand's.

Another Victorian woman novelist, Charlotte Brontë, has been compared to Sand in her own day and in recent criticism. George Eliot wrote to her friends the Brays that Lewes had met the author of *Villette,* who published under the masculine nom de plume Currer Bell, and had found her "a little plain, provincial, sickly-looking old maid. Yet what passion, what fire in her. Quite as much as in George Sand, only the clothing is less voluptuous."[6] Edward Wagenknecht, writing in 1943, commented that Brontë is "as close to George Sand as a decent British woman can come; she is a strange, northern virginal George Sand."[7] There are obvious points of comparison. Both writers used masculine noms de plume, and Brontë's first novel, *Jane Eyre,* aroused in England the same kind of anger that Sand's first books incurred. Elizabeth Rigby declared in 1848 that if a woman had written *Jane Eyre,* then she had forfeited the society of women. Evangelical writers denounced the novel. Like Sand, Brontë wrote novels to promote social reform—for example, *Shirley* concerns labor troubles in Yorkshire when laborsaving machinery is introduced. Like Sand's, Brontë's novels are often taken as reflections of her personal life: *Jane Eyre, Villette,* and *The Professor* have been read as manifestations of her hopeless love for Constantin Heger, her teacher in Belgium, who was a married man.

Writing to Lewes, who had lent her novels by Sand and Balzac, Brontë expressed a strong preference for Sand:

Fantastic, fanatical, unpractical enthusiast as she often is—far from truthful as are many of her views of life—misled, as she is apt to be, by her feelings—George Sand has had a better nature than M. de Balzac; her brain is larger, her heart warmer than his. The *Lettres d'un Voyageur* are full of the writer's self; and I never felt so strongly, as in the perusal of this work, that most of her faults spring from the excess which has prepared for her enduring regret.

But I believe her mind is of that order which disastrous experience teaches, without weakening; and in that case, the longer she lives the better she will grow. A hopeful point in all her writings is the scarcity of false French sentiment; I wish I could say its absence; but the weed flourishes here and there, even in the *Lettres*.[8]

Jane Welsh Carlyle, another Victorian woman of independent mind, also turned to French novels for comfort and vicarious experience. The relationship of Jane Welsh and Thomas Carlyle has been variously interpreted, but undoubtedly much of the tumultuous quality of their relationship stemmed from the fact that Jane was by education and temperament a strong-willed individual married to a domineering husband who thought of himself as a seer to all of England.[9] Francis Espinasse, a frequent visitor to the Carlyles, recalled that Jane was often her husband's rival in conversation and that it was better when they talked "successively rather than simultaneously, but her husband did not always allow her that alternative."[10] Once during a controversy at Chelsea, Carlyle proclaimed women as "very silly creatures" and condemned his wife's admiration of George Sand. In letters to her sister Jeannie Welsh, Jane stated that novels are an anodyne when one is in a "state of moral and physical collapse," and at one point to explain excessive sentiment in a friend, Jane wrote her husband: "But Mrs. Buller reads George Sand, like me."[11] More than once in her letters Jane Welsh used Sand as a symbol of a strong, independent mind. Commenting on the independent spirit of her dog, Nero, who ignored her after punishment, Jane wrote: "He took no notice of me after several hours. And yet he had never read George Sand's novel that dog or any sort of novels."[12]

Carlyle lectured her as he lectured all of England, to cure her of her "George Sandisms": "All of us are in horrible difficulties that look invincible, but that are not so. The deepest difficulty which also presses on us all is the sick sentimentalism we suck in with our whole nourishment, and get ingrained into the very blood of us in these miserable ages. . . . It is this that makes me so impatient of George Sand, Mazzini, and all that set of prophets."[13] Carlyle also criticized Mazzini: "Mazzini came much about us here for many years, patronized by my wife; to me very wearisome, with his incoherent Jacobinisms, George Sandisms, in spite of my love and regard for him."[14] Sand, Carlyle said, was the founder of a new religion that taught "new Phallus worship, with Sue and Balzac for prophets and Madame Sand for a virgin."[15] When Jane defended a friend of hers, a "Mrs. R", who fled to France with her lover, Jane wrote that her husband "kicked up a rumpus. . . . for my 'George Sandist' excess of humanity apropos of poor Mrs. R. My doctrine on that whole matter, he would have me know as infamous and also, my *practice* in making myself the advocate of 'W———s——it quite behove me to reform!' "[16]

On other occasions their quarrel involved literary comparisons. Carlyle praised George Eliot because he liked George Henry Lewes, who also admired Goethe and who had been kind to Carlyle in reviews. In spite of George Eliot's common-law marriage to Lewes, Carlyle considered her a seer, like himself. Jane, however, proclaimed that Eliot had been intended by nature to be the "most exemplary of women but . . . had blundered into the other camp." Carlyle retaliated by criticizing Sand's erotic novels. England, Jane replied, had little right to "cast the first stone across the Channel when she had a George of her own right there in London."[17] When Jane was jealous of Carlyle and Lady Asburton, Jane turned to Sand for a comforting phrase: "rien ne soulage comme la rhétorique," and once when she had been in a group that had included Henry Taylor and Thackeray, Jane wrote: "One brilliant person at a time, a little of him, is a charming thing; but a whole houseful of brilliant people, shining all day and every day, makes one almost of George Sand's opinion, that good honest stupidity is the best thing to associate with."[18]

Jane Carlyle's good friend Geraldine Jewsbury was more of a kindred spirit to Sand than Elizabeth Browning, George Eliot, Charlotte Brontë, or Jane Carlyle. When Jewsbury's *Zoe, The History of Two Lives* was published in 1847, it met with much the same reaction as Sand's *Jacques* and *Lélia*. Reviewers were shocked and the publisher feared that he might be arrested. Jane Carlyle had intervened to tone down some passages; yet Jane wrote her friend that "old and young roue's of the Reform Club almost go off in hysterics over—its indecency."[19] In the library of Jewsbury's hometown, Manchester, the book was kept locked in a dark cupboard because the librarian feared its circulation would injure the morals of young men.

In her private life Jewsbury, despite her efforts, was not so successful as Sand in consummating her love affairs. She nurtured a passion for Lambert Bey, a Saint-Simonian turned Mohammedan, and she carried on a long correspondence with "Q," whom she had never met but with whom Jane Carlyle and the Jewsbury family feared she would make a hasty and ill-advised marriage. She also loved Walter Mantell, who spent much of his life in New Zealand. It was a heavy blow when after a visit to England he returned to New Zealand without her. Furthermore Jewsbury was capable of demonstrating embarrassingly warm affection for members of her own sex, particularly Charlotte Cushman and Jane Carlyle. Throughout her lifetime she wrote exaggerated and lyrical sentiments to Jane, which her biographer, Susanne Howe, says she should have left to "decent oblivion where Geraldine knew they belonged. . . . They make uncomfortable reading. They were not meant for the eye of the twentieth-century reader who is so ready with his Freudian interpretation."[20]

Jewsbury had debates with Carlyle on the roles of the sexes. Carlyle argued that "a woman's natural object in the world is to *go out* and find herself some sort of *man her superior*—& obey him loyally and lovingly and make herself as much as possible into a *beautiful reflexion of him,*" to which Geraldine would reply, "The difficulty is to find a man who can be our master. . . . It is not the women who fail in docility but the men are not high enough to rule."[21] Jewsbury's article in the *Westminster Review* in 1850 was favorable to Père Enfantin of the Saint-Simonians, further illustrating her emancipated views.

Among her friends were two translators of Sand, Matilda Hays and Eliza Ashurst. It was at the Ashurst home that Joseph Mazzini spent a great deal of time when he was in England. Through him Jewsbury tried to meet Sand, sending her a copy of *Zoe,* Mazzini bearing the gift to Paris. Sand acknowledged receipt of the book in April 1845, but there is no evidence that she read it; and although Sand extended a vague invitation, Jewsbury made two visits to Paris without receiving an interview.

However, a visit by Eliza Ashurst to her French idol did not establish a relationship between emancipated women on either side of the channel. Mazzini had told Sand's English admirers that Sand did not care for England, considering it a land of snobs, everyone but Byron, and he had fled England. When Ashurst went over to change Sand's mind, Sand was not impressed and wrote Mazzini that she thought the English woman's reading of Sand's books had not been good for her. The *Foreign Quarterly* reviewer of 1841 who had warned that "self-styled emancipators of women" would accomplish nothing "beyond reducing that beautiful creation of maiden, wife and mother to a mere impure being"[22] might have used Ashurst as an example. Sand, writing to Mazzini, further characterized Ashurst as "a prude without modesty" and "very English, for the real Englishman thinks himself the finest man of the finest nation."[23] This was written after the youthful Arnold made his pilgrimage to Sand at Nohant. Sand had not yet met the Brownings, but their visits were to impress her very little.

One more emancipated woman influenced by Sand was Marie Louise de la Ramée, who wrote under the pen name Ouida. Critics considered her works beneath criticism, yet everyone from pantry-maids to peers read her. Two of Ouida's biographers, Yvonne Ffrench and Eileen Bigland, credit Sand as Ouida's inspiration for her literary creations and for her literary salon; French critics also saw Sand's influence, especially in *Idalia*.

Ouida, Jewsbury, Sand, and others are examples of what moralists expected to find when they looked to literary circles. There they could always find unconventional figures threatening the status quo. Shelley and Byron had been recent bad examples, and there was ample evidence, as Walter Houghton writes, of "immediate signs that the sexual impulse was threatening to overflow the traditional dykes; signs so ominous that men felt it could be checked only by the most severe and repressive code."[24] Mephistopheles's comment to Gretchen on the subject of free love was also applicable to England. When Gretchen protests, "that is not the custom of our race," Mephistopheles replies, "Custom or not it's what takes place."

William J. Fox, Unitarian minister and editor of the influential *Monthly Repository*,[25] separated from his wife and set up a household with Eliza Flower. Their experience of being trapped by strict divorce laws was not an isolated case. The lives of John Stuart Mill and Harriet Taylor were dogged by scandal, and Mill was sternly censured by his father for being in love with another man's wife. Even after their marriage, which followed Mr. Taylor's death by two years, the couple seldom went out into society. The long unconventional relationship of George Eliot and George Henry Lewes (which lasted from 1854 until Lewes's death in 1878) shocked society and isolated Eliot and Lewes; only their most loyal friends called on them at their home, the Priory.

There were other examples to suggest to many Victorians that England was already too close an imitation of young France: Charles Dickens, after twenty-two years of marriage and ten children, left his wife for Ellen Ternan, the actress. Other names in the literary and artistic world whose lives challenged convention were the bohemian Thornton Hunt, Charles Reade and Mrs. Seymour, John Chapman and Elizabeth Tilley, Whistler and his mistress, Bulwer-Lytton and Hortense Allart, and Wilkie Collins and his mistresses.[26] The list is impressive and could be lengthened.

Victorian judgments of Sand have to be evaluated against such a background, and one gains perspective when he remembers that all criticism of Sand did not stem from Anglo-Saxon prudery. Bertha Thomas, Sand's English biographer in the 1880s, states that the French themselves began an unwarranted, unsympathetic judgment of Sand that English critics took up. As an example Thomas quoted Renan's recollections when in his youth his ecclesiastical superiors showed him Sand emblematically portrayed as a woman in black trampling on a cross. There were other reviews that support Thomas's thesis: Capo de Feuillade, editor of *Europe Littéraire,* called for a red-hot coal to purify the lips of an author who had uttered such shameful and disgusting thoughts as were found in *Lélia.* He advised parents reading the books to lock their doors after they had sent their daughters out to play. Such topics as equality of the sexes in love shocked Lamennais, editor of *Le Monde,* in which *Lettres à Marcie* were published. When Sand proposed discussing the role of passion in a woman's life, Lamennais suspended publication of the series.

There are always the unanswered questions of to what degree Sand influenced the behavior of others or to what extent she was merely a compelling symbol at a time when women of the Victorian era loosened inhibitions to realize new freedoms. A twentieth-century reader might with some justification argue that new light needed to be shed on the "role of passion in a woman's life," especially if the Victorian woman quoted by Diane Johnson in *Lesser Lives* is at all a fair sample. Asked how she endured the odious side of marriage, she replied, "I just lie on my back and think of England."[27]

Surely to two Victorian women of talent, Elizabeth Barrett Browning and George Eliot, George Sand was an inspiration. She encouraged Mrs. Browning to break the psychotic tyranny of a father and she comforted George Eliot in flaunting the strictures of society concerning difficult divorce laws. To them and to other Victorian women with literary aspirations, Sand was a decided success, notorious or not, a woman making her reputation and earning her living by writing novels that the public took seriously.

Finally, Heinrich Heine's estimate may have been very correct: Sand's works set the world on fire, bringing warmth and light; yet they may, at the same time, have destroyed, or at least affected, "peaceful temples of innocence."

IV

The Socialist Republican: Muse of the Second Republic

> One of the four great corner-stones of Socialism and Philanthropy of the Modern World. Sainte-Beuve

George Sand's reputation in Victorian England was also influenced by her politics. Although her writings on women's rights may be considered political, this issue ran afoul of moral principles and became more than political. Besides there were additional factors that gave a strong political cast to Sand's image in England and France.

Sand's family was too involved in the history of France for her not to become involved in French politics. When Sand was a child of five, she and her mother had accompanied her father to Spain, where he was aide-de-camp to Murat during Napoleon's disastrous Spanish campaign. Her rearing by her grandmother, a lady of the old regime, made Sand conscious of the claims of the aristocracy. Yet her mother was of humble origins and through her Sand identified with the masses.

Political upheavals in France in 1830 and 1848 were attempts to complete the Revolution begun in 1789. Through Jules Sandeau and other members of the artistic set that came to Berry, Sand felt the rumbles of the romantic revolution that reverberated through the literature and politics of France. These associations encouraged her to leave a boorish husband and to seek her own freedom and self-fulfillment through literature and love. When love failed, Sand turned to politics and social reform.

Indeed one of her early lovers, Michel de Bourges, a militant republican, attempted to persuade Sand to reject love and seek the ideal in politics. Sand agreed in part but could not accept his principle of violence to accomplish social gains. She wrote:

> Let us go forward. No matter what the subtle colours of your banner so long as your companies march ever along the road that leads to the ultimate Republic. In the name of Jesus, who has upon this earth no single true apostle; in the names of Washington and Franklin, who failed to finish their work and have left us a task still to accomplish; in the name of Saint-Simon, whose sons bravely tackle the sublime and terrible problem (may God protect them.)—provide only that the good prevail.[1]

Several friendships at this time intensified Sand's political writings and activities, increasing her image as a Socialist Republican and Muse of the Second Republic. She became friends with Franz Liszt, who considered himself a Saint-Simonian, and his mistress, the Countess d'Agoult.[2] They introduced her to the Abbé Felicité de Lamennais, an unfrocked priest whose zeal to make the church a vehicle of social reform got him in trouble with Rome. She became a great admirer of Pierre Leroux, another reformer and a second-rate thinker whose teaching at an early phase of Sand's emancipation was thought by her to sum up the best of Christianity, Plato, Lamennais, Michel de Bourges, Rousseau, and Benjamin Franklin! Leroux's ideas on metempsychosis[3] were especially appealing to Sand in the

1840s. She agreed with him also on the evil of property rights, wrongs in the family structure, and the need to unite the flesh with the spirit to achieve the ideal.

Sand espoused many causes, including that of Louis Blanc, a socialist with communist sympathies, whose newspaper carried the slogan "To each according to his needs." Sainte-Beuve wrote in 1843 that Béranger, Lamennais, Sand, and Sue were the "four great corner-stones of Socialism and Philanthropy of the modern world."

Sand's novels reflected her newfound political interests. The hero of *Le Compagnon du Tour de France* (1841) is Pierre Hughenin, a humble carpenter like Jesus. *Horace* (1841) was so socialistic in tone that Buloz, the publisher, refused the manuscript. *Le Meunier d'Angibault* (1845) idealized a rustic miller, and *Le Péché de M. Antoine* (1846) preached socialistic doctrines. Four pastoral novels, which are Sand's most enduring works, preached that true values reside in lowly people: *Jeanne* (1845), *La Mare au Diable* (1846), *François le Champi* and *La Petite Fadette* (both 1849).

Chiefly it was the Revolution of 1848 that molded Sand's reputation in French politics. She came to Paris at first to look out for her adored son, Maurice, who had joined liberal forces; once in Paris, she put all of her poet's spirit and enthusiasm into the revolutionary cause. She associated with Lamartine and Tocqueville, and through the interest of Ledru-Rollin she became editor of the *Bulletin de la République*. In one letter she wrote that communism was the "true Christianity" and that communists did not destroy family and property as they were commonly thought to do. She further observed: "The masses are not Communists. Yet France will be called to be Communists before a hundred years have passed."[4]

In one revolutionary issue of the *Bulletin* in particular, Sand seemed to espouse Michel de Bourges's doctrine of violence. She wrote that if election returns did not "assure the triumph of social truth," then barricades must be built again, as they had been originally constructed during the Revolution. The election returns showed a conservative trend, and Sand's advice was seemingly taken when liberals led by Armand Barbes and Louis Blanc attempted unsuccessfully to storm the Palais-Bourbon and declare the birth of a socialist republic.

By the failure Sand saw the socialist cause was lost and withdrew to her estate at Nohant. In this spacious home, inherited from her grandmother, she continued to write, collect friends, and build a new image: the good lady of Nohant. She entered the political sphere thereafter only to intervene with the prince-president on behalf of political prisoners, many of whom because of her great prestige she was able to save from deportation or imprisonment. After the prince-president became Napoleon III, Sand interceded for political prisoners through the Empress Eugénie, who attempted to have Sand elected the first woman member of the French Academy.[5] None of these events went unnoticed in England. As early as 1835, before Sand had received widespread British recognition as a writer of novels, *Blackwood's Edinburgh Review* printed a dialogue between Sand and a friend on Talleyrand's vanity.[6] When Sand's novels were reviewed, the bias of the critic was often political as in the case of John Wilson Croker. He wrote: "Such publications pervert not only individuals but nations, and are alternately the cause and consequence of a spirit which threatens the whole fabric of a European society."[7] Occurring in Croker's 1836 review was an idea that persisted among English Tories, that Sand took her pen name from a political assassin, Karl Sand, a German student who in 1819 had shot and killed Kotzebue, a Russian agent. Public opinion in England was sharply divided: to Liberals, Karl Sand was a hero; to Conservatives, the hero was Kotzebue. Croker speculated:

> But the choice of the pseudonyme is not unimportant, and deserves a passing observation—GEORGE SAND. A *German* name can hardly have been chosen at random by a *French* writer. Why, then, *Sand?* . . . If this name was assumed as an indication of the character of the author's works, it was, to a certain degree, well chosen; but though the name of Sand is in harmony with many of these blood-stained pages, it affords no promise of the lascivious scenes, which are still more frequent. We have had, and we still have some conscientious doubts whether we should mention this author at all, but we have been determined to do so by having found *his* works in our London circulating libraries. Whether we shall have sufficient influence to put them into the *Index Expurgatorious* we know not.[8]

Croker concluded his article by speaking of his love for France and expressed conviction that France's best hope lay in the virtuous character of her present king.

The origin of Sand's pen name intrigued British critics until the 1850s and was the subject of speculation in the *London and Westminster Review* of 1836, the *Foreign Quarterly* of 1838, the *Foreign Quarterly and Colonial Review* of 1843, and by George Henry Lewes in the *Foreign Quarterly Review* of 1844; the issue subsided but the

London Society magazine in 1870 still attempted to explain the true origin.[9]

Political bias worked in Sand's favor in the case of Joseph Mazzini, Sand's greatest champion in the English press. Sand had been attracted to Mazzini for political reasons when he was a member of the Young Italy Movement, writing letters to Tocqueville and Falloux. The letters appeared in the French press about the time Mazzini had been exiled to Switzerland for political activities.[10] Sand had just fled her unhappy marriage and was still in her age of tempests. In fact she broke her resolve to see Mazzini at the time only to spare him her own "agitated soul."[11] In 1837 when Mazzini thought Switzerland too dangerous for him because of his politics, he joined a group of Italian exiles in England[12] and dabbled in literature.

It was then that he reviewed Sand's novels and boasted that he had introduced her to England. Although he condemned John Wilson Croker for his political bias, Mazzini seemed unaware of his own. Sand, he wrote, "belongs to the democratic faith; her works breathe a love of the people, and a contempt for aristocracies, great and little; she is allied by esteem and friendship with M. Lamennais and the most marked men of the rising faith."[13] In her works Sand offered solace, Mazzini stated, for anyone oppressed by the strong, for women oppressed by marriage customs, even for writers oppressed by literary traditions. Sand's followers, he wrote, looked for a new religion and knew how, if necessary, to shed blood for their ideals.[14]

Liberals going to the Continent applied to Mazzini for letters of introduction to Sand. One was the American writer Margaret Fuller, a feminist and a socialist, who probably had met Mazzini through the Carlyles. Fuller arrived in Paris in November 1846 and by means of such a letter saw Sand. She was accompanied by a Mr. and Mrs. Spring, described as "active in the cause of the poor Negroes" of America.[15]

When Mazzini finally met Sand in 1847 at Nohant he wrote Jane Carlyle how pleased he was with their literary idol, that she practiced "all the ideas of equality and love that she preaches in her novels."[16] The friendship became strained when Sand seemed to accept Napoleon III. There is no doubt that Mazzini's interest in Sand was primarily political, however much he might denounce John Wilson Croker for his political approach.

Sand's other champion, George Henry Lewes, used literary standards to judge her works far more than did any other Victorian critic; yet he too defended her politics, declaring that he knew of no dangerous social theories that she was trying to promulgate. She was, Lewes declared, a democrat who preferred Lamennais to Louis Philippe, and she was unhappy with Christianity as it was then practiced. Lewes admitted that Sand raised questions about problems to which she had no solutions, but so did the great Goethe. Lewes found Sand's socialistic *Le Meunier d'Angibault* excellent in style at a time when he felt Sand may have written herself out. The story of the miller, he said, might be read by any "female of any age, provided she have no objection to an occasional Utopian tirade. Any democratic young lady may open it without hesitation."[17]

Most reviewers were hostile. The *Eclectic Review* as early as 1840 identified Sand as "writer and politician," eight years before the Revolution of 1848, when Sand won her greatest political fame. In the pages of this dissenting magazine, which did not admire Sand for her politics or her morals, G.W.M. Reynolds wrote:

> The revolution of July made the Baroness Dudevant a writer. A little more than eight years ago she began to contemplate that terrible ebullition of an outraged spirit of the heroes of the barricades, she imperceptibly inhaled the generous fervor of enthusiasm herself. Her mind expanded as she contemplated the progressive march of liberty; and she determined that the course of intelligence should move at an equal pace and in a parallel line. Her ideas were thus formed by a great political event which could not fail to render the writings of its disciple striking and peculiar.[18]

An *Athenaeum* review in 1841 of Sand's *A Winter in the South of Europe* praised descriptive passages but pointedly omitted references to Sand's "speculative matter," explaining that Sand "loses no opportunity to preach the new doctrines of M. de Lamennais and his sect."[19]

Thackeray, in an article entitled "Balzac on the Newspapers of Paris," commented about a picture of Leroux: "Observe the agitated frenzy of M. Pierre Leroux, with divorce, dissolution, disruption, George Sandism in every part of his aspect."[20]

The conservative *Foreign and Colonial Review* echoed sentiments previously stated by Croker in the *Quarterly Review;* there was, the reviewer wrote, such an interplay between a national literature and a nation's politics that a historian and "contemporary inquirer" had an obligation to investigate French novels in order to warn the British public. Thus he had waded through "with fatiguing labor" thirty-three of Sand's volumes. What he found there was a total lack of morals and a championing of suicide, lying, and murder. Sand, the critic charged, equated Socrates and Christ and admired Christianity only as something to keep ignorant masses happy until they could be educated to better things. He was thankful that England had been spared France's fate, for he doubted whether France could any longer be called a Christian nation. France, he said, was a nation where "every flitting phantom, and every fever-engendered monster, the hideous creation of the diseased brain, . . . passes with phantasmagoric rapidity before being instantly reflected on the surface of the equally rapidly varying literature of the day."[21]

Sand was injected into political commentary even when there seemed to be no need. When the issue was being discussed whether Parliament should cease calling itself a Christian body so that Jewish members might be admitted, a Tory critic writing in the *Quarterly Review* disagreed with Macaulay that a man's Christianity had nothing to do with his fitness to be a legislator. The Tory asked what standards were to be substituted if Christian standards were set aside and added sarcastically that perhaps England might see the new Messiah whom the Pantheists were always predicting; then Englishmen could practice the new religion which recognized virtue and vice as developments of human nature "equally respectable" and a new code of morals in which "adultery and incest are to be cardinal virtues, and marriage the unpardonable sin." This comment triggered a reference to Sand, and a footnote added:

See the writings *passim* of that great apostle of pantheism, the 'semivir obscoenus' of France, George Sand, whose philosophy, after all, is nothing but Rousseau modernised, and she herself Jean Jacques, we were about to say, in petticoats, but we believe she most frequently discards those vulgar remnants of the ancient regime. If we are to believe the newspaper-advertisements, an attempt is now making by an English *editrix,* assisted among others by a beneficed clergyman of the English Church, to circulate these productions here in English translation—*omitting the obscenity*. We denounce this scheme, not from any wish to widen the original flood of pollution—God forbid—but in confidence that the public would not tolerate the undisguised poison, while the *modest* emendation is a smuggler's attempt to conceal the real nature of his infamous cargo—the inevitable moral consequences of Madame Dudevant's avowed creed. If there is really such a person as "the Rev. E. R. Larkin, Chaplin to Lord Monson, and Rector of Burton by Lincoln," the open connexion of his name with 'The Works of George Sand' appears to us a strange phenomenon.[22]

The above article appeared in 1847, eleven years after Croker's first "alarm" against Sand, to use Mazzini's term. That same year Gustave Masson, writing in the *Wesleyan Methodist,* responded to editor Douglas Jerrold of *Weekly Newspaper* that the Methodist magazine had ignored Sand in its literary reviews not because of the content of her works but primarily because Sand was a political figure and a social reformer.

It was T. C. Sandars with his usual commonsense approach who best assessed Sand's politics for the Victorians: she built no system, he said; besides evil in the convention of marriage, she chiefly railed out against the world's treatment of the poor, but when the reader looked for suggestions for correcting evils in present institutions he became lost in the "beautiful but obscure language of feminine philosophy."[23] Her socialism he found nonsensical: manufacturers were always corrupt, and workers never robbed their proprietors. Yet he found that Sand's common sense saved her: her belief that rewards for socialism would come in the distant future—as in *La Péché de M. Antoine,* where the marquis plans a park for peasants when they have all become pious! Lastly Sandars approved of Sand's belief that the individual was capable of rapid change even if society was not.

Sandars was astute in recognizing that Sand's socialism was too visionary for the average Englishman, even those who had the desire to help the needy en masse and those who admired Sand's own generosity toward the poor. No doubt much of Sand's socialism, growing out of mystical views of Leroux and Lamennais, offended many Victorians just as the religious views of the Saint-Simonians offended John Stuart Mill. Still, Sand's novels of the 1840s with a social purpose had counterparts in novels like Frances Trollope's *Michael Armstrong, The Factory Boy* (1840), Elizabeth Gaskell's *Mary Barton* (1848), Charlotte Brontë's *Shirley* (1849), Charles Kingsley's *Alton Locke* (1840), Geraldine Jewsbury's *Marion Withers* (1851), Charles Dickens's *Hard Times* (1855), and George Eliot's *Felix Holt* (1866). This list of course could be lengthened considerably, for Victorian novelists at times seem obsessed with social problems. Although this tendency cannot be traced to Sand's influence, many Victorian novelists admired Sand, and her works dealing with social problems endeared her to them.

George Eliot was one who shared many of Sand's political views. She admired the Revolution of 1848, which Tennyson (probably closer to typical Victorian reaction) called the "crisis of the mad and bloody folly on the Seine." George Eliot also shared views similar to Sand's on the value of the French working class. In February of 1848 Eliot described the "spirit of the French people charged with electricity" and stated that the French masses were vitally interested in social problems, much more so than their "equivalents" in English society. Eliot may have got this idea from Sand, or she may have borrowed it from Sand's friend Louis Blanc.[24] In 1852 Eliot wrote Sara Hennell that she had been hearing Leroux, who had escaped to England after the coup d'etat of 1851, and she described him as a "dreamy genius" who "has found the true point which is to unite the love of self and of one's neighbor." She identified Leroux further: "George Sand has dedicated some of her books to him."[25]

There is evidence that John Stuart Mill took Sand seriously as a political figure. He sent her a copy of his *The Principles of Political Economy* (1848) because he sympathized with her social theories, some of which he hoped to correct. Another commentator on French politics, Elizabeth Barrett Browning, wrote two letters in 1849 to her author-friend Mary Mitford concerning Margaret Fuller's visit to Sand. In these letters she commented on the effect that French politics were having on French writers, especially Dumas and Sand, implying that both writers were much involved in the political scene.[26] Three years later Mrs. Browning defended her idol against the charge that Sand had succumbed before the power and influence of Napoleon III; but then Mrs. Browning always defended

Sand, whether her politics appeared to be communist or monarchist, for the author of *Aurora Leigh* shared with Sand an intense desire for social reform.

Sand's political views were a great part of her appeal to Matthew Arnold. When he was at Oxford, Sand seemed to him and his associates, Arthur Hugh Clough, Theodore Walrond, and Thomas Arnold, his younger brother, to be "the incarnation of a new spirit of revolt and renovation."[27] In 1845 Arnold wrote to Clough quoting from memory a speech of Sand's heroine Indiana, in which she describes a religious attitude that Arnold felt represented a true idealistic spirit even if it might encourage revolution:

> If a Being so vast deigned to take any Part in our miserable interests, it would be to raise up the weak, and to beat down the Strong:—it would be to pass his heavy hand over our heads, and to level them like the waters of the Sea:—to say to the Slave, "Throw away thy chain,"—and to the strong, "Bear thy Brother's burden: for I have given him strength and wisdom and thou shalt oppress him no longer."[28]

Arnold contrasted this attitude with the orthodox and pious teachings of Hannah More, whom he disliked intensely; yet he wrote, almost cryptically, that if Sand's teachings were organized into law, they would lose much of their effectiveness:

> But never without a Pang do I hear of the growing Popularity of a strong minded writer. Then I know what hideosities [,] what Solecisms, what Lies, what crudities, what distortions, what Grimaces, what affectations, what disown[m]ent of the Trimmer-X-Hannah-More-typed spirit they are of, I shall hear and see amongst the born-to-be-tight-laced of my friends and

acquaintance: then I know the strong minded writer will lose his self-knowledge, and talk of his usefulness and imagine himself a Reformer, instead of an Exhibition. Rightly considered, a Code-G.-Sand would make G.Sands impossible.[29]

There is evidence that in 1848 Arnold was displeased by Sand's political activity. She had written two letters for the newspaper *La Vraie République* expressing disapproval of the new government because it allowed the provinces to be controlled by the people of Paris. Arnold wrote Clough: "I have G. Sand's letter—do you want it? I do not like it so well as at first. For my soul I cannot *understand* this violent praise of the people. I praise a fagot where-of the several twigs are nought: but a *people*?" A month later, when Arnold had still not sent Sand's letter to Clough, he concluded another letter to Clough, "Expectandum est.—I send G.S."[30] The following month he transmitted to Clough the false rumor, reported in the London *Times,* that Sand had been arrested for her political activities.

Although Arnold's reactions to Sand will be discussed at length in a later chapter, his response to her political views can be found in his anniversary essay on Sand, published in the *Fortnightly Review* in 1877. Choosing Sand's themes that pleased him most, Arnold discussed her idea that love is the basis of social life. He saw, says Lionel Trilling, that the average Englishman would accept this doctrine if it were kept general but would shy away from the idea if "love" meant complete social equality. Arnold directed the remaining efforts of his life to get his countrymen to move closer to the doctrine and fear it less: he defined civilization as the humanization of man in society through an understanding of power of conduct, the power of intellect and knowledge, the power of beauty, and the power of social life and manners. This civilization, which Arnold called *expansion,* consisted of the brand of liberty and equality that he and Sand admired; and Arnold believed that as long as the present inequality remained, England would remain uncivilized.[31]

In 1882, as Arnold drew to the close of his life, he gained a new interest in Sand through her mystical novel *Spiridion* and copied thirty-four passages from the work into his *Note-Books*. The last passage that he copied from Sand had an optimistic conclusion about society: in the passage Florence asks Jacques if the world is still far from the "shining summit." Jacques replies that the answer is God's secret, but their world is much closer to perfection than that of "all the people who preceded us."[32]

A major evidence of Sand's stature as a political figure among the Victorians is found in the first English biography of her, by Bertha Thomas, published in 1883. Much of the biography develops Sand's career in politics. The biographer attributes Sand's initial revolt in 1831 to current political changes. Two of the twelve chapters are entitled "Solitude, Society and Socialism" and "Novelist and Politician." Mrs. Thomas attempts to justify most of Sand's actions that had shocked Englishmen; she attempts to explain *Bulletin Number 16* as stemming from Sand's naïveté, and she points out that Sand denied any participation in or sympathy with the insurrection of 15 May 1848.

Two stories that Mrs. Thomas relates about Sand's political career have an appealing quality. One concerns the May 15 insurrection, when someone pointed out a female orator who was haranguing the crowd from the lower window of a cafe. When Sand asked who the woman was, she was assured that the female orator inflaming the crowd was none other than George Sand herself. Another story proves that Sand was remembered by the socialists long after she had retired from politics to Nohant. During Napoleon III's war with Prussia, on 11 October 1870, two balloons attempted to escape besieged Paris; one of the balloons the socialists named "George Sand"; the other they named "Armand Barbès," for the socialist leader. The balloon named for Sand was unsuccessful in its flight; it descended with difficulty, although all on board, including some Americans, were rescued. On the "Armand Barbès" was Gambetta, who was safely carried to Tours.

Mrs. Thomas points out that Sand's socialism had as its aim fairly mild reforms with which English politicians were preoccupied: free education for the poor and a fair adjustment of relations between capital and labor. As George Henry Lewes argued concerning Sand's morals, Mrs. Thomas contends that Sand's political notoriety was exaggerated and that after the failure of the new republic in 1848 she turned to a safe religious socialism, which had as its aim the establishment of a utopia in the distant future.

There is evidence that Sand maintained her optimistic political idealism in spite of expedient pragmatism of politicians and the hostility of some of her critics. Nowhere is her continued optimism better revealed than in a letter to Flaubert, written after the defeat of France in the Franco-Prussian War:

> This is no time to be sick, old troubadour, no time to grumble. What we've got to do is cough, wipe our noses, get well, and declare that France is mad, humanity stupid, and we ourselves no more than a lot of badly designed and half-bungled animals. . . . That's all true enough; still, we have got to go on being in love with ourselves, the species to which we belong, and, most of all, our friends. . . . Maybe this chronic state of indignation is one of the necessary conditions of your continued existence: I know that it would be the death of me! . . . Is it possible, you ask, to live in peace when the human race is so absurd? Speaking for myself, I am prepared to submit to the conditions, reflecting the while that I, perhaps, am no less absurd, and that it is about time I began to think how to improve myself.[33]

As T. C. Sandars pointed out, Sand believed the individual was capable of sudden change even if society was not. Her abiding faith in the capacity of the individual to move rapidly while society merely stumbled toward a higher goal is one of those qualities that gave Sand great appeal to Matthew Arnold, who was willing to overlook much because of this one quality.

Generally, Victorian critics who were hostile to Sand's moral code opposed her politics; and those who defended her morality, feeling that her bad reputation was undeserved and greatly exaggerated, also defended her political views. Later in the century Leslie Stephen, who was neither Sand's advocate nor her enemy, felt that her politics got in the way of art. Writing to C. E. Norton, he called Sand's *Histoire de ma Vie* "about the best autobiography I have ever read," but he objected to Sand's patriotic sentiments: "She is in a rather stupid bit of her story, and has just disgusted me by saying that all the armies of Europe could not have put down the French if they had not had the royalist party amongst them. I hate all patriotic sentiments. They mean vulgar brag; and here is a woman, who is supposed to be a model of taste, reduced by her idiotic patriotisms into talking stuff fit for X.Y.'s (an officer's) mess—i.e., a French X.Y."[34]

Perhaps all Stephen did was restate what every writer about Sand had recognized, whether he was her friend or foe: she believed that the artist needed to be involved with social problems and politics, an idea she shared with a great many Victorians. Although to a lesser degree than her ideas on love and marriage, her political ideas helped shape her literary reputation in England.

V

The Literary Artist: Nineteenth-Century Sappho

Her prose stirs you like music. — John Stuart Mill

We would say with Theocritus, that her music is more lulling than the sound of water flowing from a rock.
G. H. Lewes

Although Sand's fame among the Victorians rested on many bases, the firmest one of all was their appreciation of her literary talent. Victorians admired her as a stylist; they had a high regard for her characterizations and reveled in her nature descriptions; many preferred her brand of romanticism to the rising realism of the day and felt that she had a message for the age.

Two of her admirers, Mazzini and Lewes, helped set the tone of criticism by their extravagant praise. Mazzini ranked Sand high among contemporary French writers, and George Henry Lewes wrote: "All the beauties of the prose literature of the seventeenth century, put together, would not equal the prose of George Sand. . . . I would say that of all which has been written of the same kind by all the writers of other epochs, I see nothing that can for an instant be compared to certain descriptions—to whole volumes of George Sand."[1] T. C. Sandars was attracted to Sand's appreciation of beauty, reflected in her language as she dealt in self-analysis. A *London Society* writer deprecated critics who saw in Sand "the rhythm of Homer and Virgil, the verve of Juvenal, the sublimity of Dante and the sarcasm of Byron,"[2] yet the comment reveals how extravagant their praise often was. Elizabeth Barrett commented to Mary Mitford that she could read a book "upon a walking stick," if it were written eloquently.

> Style is music to me. I cannot help my pleasure in the beauty of it. Now, to my mind and ear too, the bare *french* of that wonderful genius Victor Hugo, and of this brilliant monstrous woman Madame Dudevant, is french *transfigured*. . . . It is not french—it is french no more. We recognize nothing like it in Voltaire—and the previous (so-called) classical writers. It is too sweet for french,—and too strong—and above all, too numerous. It is something like the "voice of the charmer" to me.[3]

Elizabeth called Sand the greatest female genius since Sappho.

John Ruskin labeled Sand "often immoral always beautiful." John Stuart Mill refused to agree with John Morley that Sand's style was the "high-water mark of prose, but yet could not name anybody higher," and admitted that "her prose stirs you like music." The Victorians were joined by readers in other nations who in their praise stopped often just short of idolatry. Henry James wrote that Sand's style had the "odor of hawthorn and the wild honeysuckle." Ernest Renan called Sand the "Aeolian harp of our times," and Alexandre Dumas fils commented that Sand "thinks like Montaigne, dreams like Ossian, writes like Jean Jacques."[4] Turgenev in 1858 made a pilgrimage to Nohant to pay his respects.

Sand's description of nature endeared her to many Victorians, among them Matthew Arnold and her early reviewer Mary Margaret Busk. Even uncomplimentary reviewers, such as one in the *Foreign and Colonial Quarterly Review* of 1843, praised Sand's feeling for nature. The praise endured: a *Blackwood's* reviewer in 1876 writing on "Country Life" was compelled to refer to Sand's idealized view of rural living; although A. Innes Shand, writing also for *Blackwood's* in 1877, found Sand's peasants so idealized that he feared her friends who were inspired by her novels to visit the Berry countryside would never recognize the peasants once they got there. Two critics, Frederic W. H. Myers and Matthew Arnold, selected *Valvèdre* as a superb example of Sand's handling of nature, and John Addington Symonds chose the same novel as his favorite and praised Sand's nature description, finding this "devotion to nature for her own sake and the essential freedom which we regard as the central point of Elizabethanism."[5]

Sand's distinct ability to paint characters also won the praise of many Victorians. Mrs. Busk admired the grandmother in *Valentine* and the rough veterans of the Imperial Army as they appeared in *Jacques*. A critic in the *British and Foreign Review* maintained that poetry was not dead as long as an author could create a heroine like the one in *André;* he admired Marcasse the rat-catcher, also from *André,* and commented: "Nor have the characters in which George Sand is successful that fault so largely destructive of the reader's trustful intimacy with so many of the personages of contemporary French novels. They are not over-wrought; their passions develope themselves in simple and dramatic dialogues; their action is well noted down without a stiff and trammeling minuteness; there is life in their repose."[6]

George Henry Lewes found Sand a poet who created characters while Balzac was a philosopher who merely criticized his. Later when Lewes stated that Sand was prostituting her talent, he still felt she could depict characters well, especially old men and rascals among young men. T. C. Sandars, like Lewes, admired the rascals and saw them as foils for other characters.

Of all the Victorian critics, George Henry Lewes used criteria that are most respected today. Joseph Mazzini treated her too much like a priestess of a new religious cult, a priestess whose politics he admired. Lewes came closest to meeting Arnold's criterion of "disinterestedness," and two lengthy articles in the *Foreign Quarterly Review* in July 1844 and April 1846[7] did much to establish Sand's literary reputation in Victorian England.

Lewes's 1844 review came when Balzac and Sand had edited their complete works, six volumes from Balzac, sixteen from Sand. Lewes compared the two writers from three points of view: the author as moralist, the author as artist, the author as entertainer. Sand emerged superior in all three categories. She was moral because she spoke what she believed to be the truth; if there were painful passages, they reflected the evil of her times. On the other hand, Lewes charged, Balzac made adultery seem the "general condition of society." As an artist, Lewes found Sand superior to Balzac in her style, her characterizations, and in what Lewes called her "poetic conceptions." Balzac he found artificial (as when he described nature as a woman dressed for a ball) and he disliked Balzac's attention to detail: "He cannot mention a single room in the house, but he must instantly make an inventory of the furniture, as if with an eye to distraining for rent." Lewes summed up: Balzac gave inventory; Sand gave emotion. *Lélia* he found the "most extraordinary piece of writing extant . . . alternately a hymn on the majesty of nature and an elegy on the nothingness of life." He then quoted a long passage in the original French, commenting that he never encountered such passages without "feeling as at an open window on a fair May morn." He declared her style "perhaps the most beautiful ever written by a French author." In his third category, the artist as entertainer, Lewes admitted Sand and Balzac both had wide reputations but Sand was greater than Balzac because she was "moral," and he explained that by moral he did not mean "sermons in the style of Hannah More." He probably meant something like what Longinus meant in "On the Sublime" when he referred to the "universal theme" that makes up a great literary work. In this Lewes would agree with Matthew Arnold, who was also indebted to Longinus. Arnold found Sand "moral" in this sense, not trivial and topical like Balzac.

In contrasting Balzac and Sand, Lewes revealed a dominant Victorian preference for romanticism over realism. Mazzini shared this Victorian bias. He said that realists like Balzac took as their motto the same cry that was heard in the streets of Naples at the time of a plague: "Have you any dead? Show lights in your windows." The realists, he claimed, took all that was dead, unclean, and unhealthy in society and showed it to view. Such a practice, he said, "unpoeticized" virtue, corrupted the imagination, promoted unbelief, and encouraged suicide.

Lewes and Mazzini had noteworthy Victorians on their

side: Elizabeth Browning, who found Balzac deeper in the mire than Sand; John Ruskin, who did not like realistic fiction, which he felt developed in London suburbs "feeding the demands of the rows of similar brick houses which branch in devouring cancer round every manufacturing town," and who consequently found George Eliot the worst kind of Cockney realist.[8] Matthew Arnold felt Sand would establish superiority over Balzac; and Charlotte Brontë preferred Sand to Balzac. As late as 1880, Andrew Lang wrote, "If the battle between the crocodile of Realism and the catawampus of Romance is to be fought out to the bitter end—why in the Ragnarôk [in Norse mythology, the final destruction of the world], I am on the side of the catawampus."[9]

Many Victorians preferred the "catawampus" because they felt the romantic style best expressed a search for the ideal instead of the corrupt and dying side of society. Sand herself saw the conflict and wrote to Flaubert in 1866: "Maybe our sickness was more valuable than the reaction that followed it; than this craving for money, than this search for pleasures untouched by the ideal, than all this unchecked ambition. They do not seem to me to prove that this century has recovered its health."[10]

The Victorian conviction that their age was sick resulted in a characteristic anxiety and melancholia. Arnold speaks of "this strange disease of modern life." Tennyson's poetry is profoundly melancholic. John Stuart Mill relates in his *Autobiography* how he escaped near mental collapse through the reading of literature. Carlyle in *Sartor Resartus* documents a struggle with The Everlasting No. The desire to escape the anxiety and melancholia of the age made many Victorians turn to Sand's romantic search for the ideal, seeking in her works a message to relieve their spiritual malaise.

Most of Sand's biographies record a passage that Sand wrote in English when she was sixteen: "Written *at Nohant, upon my window, at the setting of the sun, 1820:* Go fading Sun. . . . Evening descends to bring melancholy on the landscape. With thy return, beautiful light, Nature will find again mirth and beauty, but joy will never comfort my soul."[11] While this may be a mere adolescent expression and enjoyment of weltschmerz at a low threshold of pain, to her admirers Sand became a child of the century in search of the ideal, seeking a formula for joy; as Matthew Arnold put it, his age needed "joy, but joy whose grounds are true" ("Obermann Once More," ll. 237–238).

Early in the century Mazzini stressed this quality of Sand's:

> I do not speak of glory, which, whatever has been done to prevent it, has crowned her; I know well that she values it but little. I do not even speak of something much more precious,—of the small number of chosen souls, the initiated and precursive of every country, who communicate with her from afar, whom her voice encourages and consoles, who rise up stronger from the perusal of her works, and follow all her steps with love and admiration.[12]

He gave his own personal testimony, citing what Sand's *Lettres d'un Voyageur* had meant to him:

> It was in 1836 that I first met with these "Letters," . . . My dearest friend had perished in the prisons of Charles Albert; others were condemned to linger there for twenty years; others

were dying the slow death of the soul. . . . I had no longer faith in men; no longer faith in myself. I still believed in God, and had faith in the future of my country; but from time to time doubt swept across my soul with icy wings. . . . I was about to be chased from a land Switzerland which I had learned to love as my second country. This book was to me a friend; a consolation. This sisterly voice, its accents broken by suffering, yet having strength to speak words of encouragement and hope to those "who were yet wandering amid storm and darkness," was sweet to me as is the cradle song to a weeping child. Many others have felt, many will doubtless feel, all I felt then. Travellers themselves through different paths, they will learn from these "Letters" where doubt and discouragement may lead them; and learn also how to regain strength and hope . . . "and the call of a friendly voice, from the height of the next hill, as they ascend the steeps of the lofty mountain," will be to them also, I doubt not, an encouragement and a consolation.[13]

Charlotte Brontë had a similar emotional response to the *Lettres,* and George Eliot wrote her friend Sara Hennell that she hoped Sand's *Lettres* "will do you as much good as they do me."[14]

T. C. Sandars praised Sand's "noble passion" and defined it as "that which elevates us and strengthens us in beauty of sentiment and grandeur of ideas."[15] This "strengthening" was what endeared Sand to Jane Carlyle, Elizabeth Browning, and Matthew Arnold. Balzac recognized the "noble passion" and argued that the foolish things she had done should be to her credit in "the eyes of beautiful and noble souls."[16]

Recognizing Sand's appeal and the need for her kind of romantic search to help cure the sickness of the age, Hippolyte Taine wrote Sand in 1872, just four years before her death:

> If only for our sakes, you must look after yourself for many years to come. Please give us, in addition to what you may be planning in head and heart, some such work as I once asked of you, more popular in tone, more vivid. It should be a sermon and an exhortation for men who have been bruised and wounded, but the tone of it must be that of a rousing call, of the encouragement for which all France is waiting. It is not a social thesis that her people demand, nor yet a moral one. In fact, it is not a thesis at all of which they stand in need, but the sound of frank and generous voices, the voices of maitre Favilla, of Champi, or Villemer. They want to be persuaded that there is an heroic world still within their reach, and that the world in which they live could, if only they would stand tiptoe, be made to resemble it.[17]

To stand tiptoe was the experience that Sand afforded many of her readers, and this appeal was a considerable part of her popularity. Although she was admired as one of the first emancipated women and as a political symbol, she was equally admired for her style, her characterization, her nature descriptions, and her search for the ideal. In that search she touched some of the most influential minds of her times, making the heroic seem still possible in an age of the antihero.

VI

A Few Chosen Souls: The Brownings

True genius but true woman! dost deny
The woman's nature with a manly scorn,
Elizabeth Barrett, "To George Sand"

When Mazzini referred to the "small number of chosen souls, the initiative and precursive of every country," he could have included Elizabeth Barrett. No Victorian followed Sand's activities with greater love and admiration. As an example of a free spirit Sand influenced Elizabeth Barrett in her resolve to escape her father's tyranny at Wimpole Street. As a literary figure Sand influenced her in the composition of *Aurora Leigh* in 1856, a long poem about social reform, the heroine of which is named for Sand.

Elizabeth began to read Sand after she returned from Torquay, where she had gone for her health in 1838, and she eventually completed at least eleven of Sand's books, including the earlier controversial ones (*Indiana, Jacques, Consuelo, La Comtesse de Rudolstadt, André, Leone Leoni, Jeanne, La Péché de M. Antoine, Les Maîtres Mosaïstes, Le Meunier d'Angibault,* and *Histoire de ma Vie*). She tried to read the controversial *Lélia* but could not tolerate some of the passages, although usually she was very tolerant, as this letter to her friend Mary Mitford shows:

Keep my secret—but I have been reading lately a good deal of the new French literature. Not that I would let it loose in this house, no, nor in any other—but I was curious beyond the patience of my Eve-ship; and besides grew so interested in France and the French through my long apprentice ship to the old Memoirs that I felt pricked to the heart to know all about the posterity of my heroes and heroines. And besides I live out of the world altogether, and am lonely enough and old enough and sad enough and experienced enough in every sort of good and bad reading, not to be hurt personally by a French superfluity of bad. That however is my apology. It shows peradventure a suspiciousness of conscience—and it might have been franker and plainer to have just said, "I was curious and a woman." The end remaining the same . . . that I have been reading these French books.[1]

Miss Mitford proved to be a kindred spirit in her esteem for Sand, and Elizabeth was delighted by her sympathy. A later exchange of letters (about one each week) brought comparisons of Sand with Victor Hugo, Rousseau, and Balzac, comparisons from which Sand always emerged the superior writer. When Miss Mitford objected to the sensuality of *Jacques,* Elizabeth defended the book because of its style. Once Elizabeth explained she had not read *André,* not because "it isn't naughty enough for me," but merely because it was absent from Mr. Saunder's library.[2] In still another letter Elizabeth Barrett defended French women writers, Madame Dudevant, Madame de Sévigné, and Madame Ducier.

In August 1844 Elizabeth published in two volumes her third major publication, simply entitled *Poems.*[3] In it she referred to a rising young poet, Robert Browning, placing him in the company of Spenser, Petrarch, Wordsworth, and Tennyson. Since Browning's reputation at the time was far short of Tennyson's, Browning was pleased and began a correspondence with Elizabeth that led to courtship and marriage. In that same volume were two sonnets dedicated to Sand:

To George Sand

A Desire

Thou large-brained woman and large-hearted man,
Self-called George Sand! whose soul, amid the lions
Of thy tumultous senses, moans defiance
And answers roar for roar, as spirits can:
I would some mild miraculous thunder ran
Above the applauded circus, in appliance
Of thine own nobler nature's strength and science,
Drawing two pinions, white as wings of swan,
From thy strong shoulders, to amaze the place
With holier light! that thou to woman's claim,
And man's mightst join beside the angel's grace
Of a pure genius sanctified from blame,
Till child and maiden pressed to thine embrace
To kiss upon thy lips a stainless fame.

A Recognition

True genius, but true woman! dost deny
The woman's nature with a manly scorn,
And break away the gauds and armlets worn
By weaker women in captivity?
Ah, vain denial that revolted cry
Is sobbed in by a woman's voice forlorn—
Thy woman's hair, my sister, all unshorn
Floats back dishevelled strength in agony,
Disproving thy man's name: and while before
The world thou burnest in a poet-fire
We see thy woman-heart beat evermore
Through the large flame. Beat purer, heart,
    and higher,
Till God unsex thee on the heavenly shore
Where unincarnate spirits purely aspire!

Miller thinks the lion image may be an echo of a phrase in Jules Janin's review of Sand in the *Athenaeum,* in which he called *Lélia,* "an abominable creature . . . who goes looking like a lioness after the senses in which she is deficient." Obviously the sonnets will not bear too close critical scrutiny, but they are convincing as evidence of Elizabeth's boldness in dedicating the sonnets to such a controversial figure.

Elizabeth wrote Miss Mitford of her boldness: "Mr. Kenyon told me I was a 'daring person' for the introduction of those sonnets. He has heard an able man say at his table . . . that no modest woman would or ought to confess to an acquaintance with the works of George Sand." She had thought of writing Sand "my whole mind to her of her works" and longed for a letter from Sand "though it smelt of a cigar."[4] She also plotted to send a copy of her *Poems* to Sand through John Kenyon, but the plan fell through because of Kenyon's lack of cooperation. She spoke of her father's lack of understanding of her bold curiosity about books. He did keep *Don Juan* and the *Nouvelle Héloïse* "locked up from wandering eyes," and Elizabeth felt he would as soon give them to her as prussic acid if she were thirsty.

Elizabeth continued to compare Sand favorably with other literary figures, enlarging the spectrum to include Dickens, Eugene Sue, Paul de Kock, and Charles de Bernard. When she considered moral charges that were often made against French writers, Elizabeth declared Sand's "wickedness . . . of a higher order."[5]

In September 1846 Elizabeth married the young poet she referred to as "King of the mystics,"[6] Robert Browning, who at the time ranked beneath her in fame and fortune. Wordsworth's comment was "I trust that it will be a happy union, not doubting that they will speak more intelligibly to each other than (not withstanding their abilities) they have yet done to the public."[7]

During the next three idyllic years spent in Pisa and then Florence, Elizabeth was reading all the French novels she could acquire. She wrote Miss Mitford that Robert and she were reading Sand together and that he was "in an enthusiasm" about *André*.[8] Although he disliked Elizabeth's fascination with mesmerism and her advocacy of Napoleon III, Robert found himself involved in his wife's interests. Certainly Sand was one of them.

The Brownings and their son left Casa Guidi in May 1851 for a tour of Northern Italy, Switzerland, and Paris before returning to London, where they received visits from the literary greats, including Tennyson. But Elizabeth's father continued to ignore the happy couple; of the Barretts only a sister, Arabella, and a brother, George, treated them with cordiality. When the Brownings left for Paris in September 1851 Carlyle traveled with them, and through him the Brownings got a letter from Mazzini introducing them to Sand.

Carlyle wrote Browning in October concerning this letter; he was more generous in his comments than when at home he talked about Sand to Jane Welsh:

> Mazzini can at once afford you and Mrs. Browning, without any difficulty, the required introduction to Madame Dudevant; only he says this sublime High Priestess of Anarchy is seldom now in Paris, only when there is some Play coming out or the like: so you will require to be on the outlook for her advent,

if you do not like to run out some time by railway (if there is a rail), and see her among her rustic neighbors—within sound of the "Church Bell" she has lately *christened* at her Cure's request. After all I participate in your liking for the melody that runs thro' that strange 'beautiful incontinent' soul—a *Modern* Magdalen, with the "seven devils" most likely still in her! At any rate, the introduction is most ready, the instant you write me for it.[9]

Browning responded, mentioning a new area of creativity, playwriting, into which Sand had now moved not too successfully.

Well, for Mazzini, I and my wife thank him very heartily: such a letter as you promise, will oblige us greatly, and I shall no doubt be able to find out, from people here, the best way of bringing it to bear with effect on the great person. We heard quantities about her the other night—from what may possibly be an authentic source—how she has grown visibly aged of a sudden (like Mephistopheles at the Brocken when he says he finds people ripe for the last day), and is getting more resigned to it than she had expected, seeing that with youth go "a Hell of Passions"—(which is all she knows about it). Meanwhile, the next best thing to youth, and the Hell and so on, is found to be strenuous play-writing. She writes in the country and her friends rehearse, test effects, prophesy of hits or misses of the Paris auditory; whereat she takes heart and writes again, points this, blunts that: one might as well or better, try and make articles for Chapman's Review, certainly![10]

As usual with any event, Elizabeth recorded it in a letter to Miss Mitford. The letter shows how closely she followed Sand's personal affairs: "I hear that George Sand is seldom in Paris now. She had devoted herself to play writing, and employs a houseful of men, her son's friends and her own, in acting privately with her what she writes—trying it on a home stage before she tries it at Paris. Her son is a very ordinary young man of three-and-twenty, but she is fond of him."[11]

Two weeks later she wrote that they had received the promised letter of introduction:

We have a letter for George Sand (directed à Madame George Sand) from Mazzini, and we hear that she is to be in Paris within twelve days. Then we must make a rush and present it, for her stay here is not likely to be long, and I would not miss seeing her for a great deal, though I have not read one of her late dramas, and only by faith understand that her wonderful genius has conquered new kingdoms. Her last romance "Le Chateau des Desserts" is treated disdainfully in the 'Athenaeum.' I have not read *that* even, but Mr. Chorley is apt to be cold towards French writers and I don't expect his judgment as final therefore.[12]

The much longed for meeting took place finally on 14 February when the Brownings called on Sand at 3 Rue Racine. Elizabeth lost no time in describing the event in great detail in a letter, this time to John Kenyon. The letter reads in part

Whom do you think I saw yesterday? George Sand! Oh, I have been in such fear about it! It's the most difficult thing to get access to her, and, notwithstanding our letter from Mazzini, we were assured on all sides that she would not see us. She has been persecuted by book-makers—run to ground by the race, and, after having quite lost her on her former visit to Paris, it was in half despair that we seized on an opportunity of committing our letter of introduction to a friend of a friend of hers, who promised to put it into her own hands. With the letter I wrote a little note—I writing, as I was the woman, and both of us signing it. To my delight, we had an answer by the next day's post, gracious and graceful, desiring us to call on her last Sunday. So we went. Robert let me at last, though I had a struggle for even that, the air being rather oversharp for me. But I represented to him that one might as well lose one's life as one's peace of mind for ever, and if I lost seeing her I should with difficulty get over it. So I put on my respirator, smothered myself with furs, and, in a close carriage, did not run much risk after all.

She described Sand's appearance, noting the Jewish characteristics that one can observe in some of the pictures of Sand in old age:

She received us very kindly, with hand stretched out, which I, with a natural emotion (I assure you my heart beat), stooped and kissed, when she said quickly, 'Mais non, je ne veux pas,' and kissed my lips. She is somewhat large for her height—not tall—and was dressed with great nicety in a sort of grey serge gown and jacket, made after the ruling fashion just now, and fastened up to the throat, plain linen collarette and sleeves. Her hair was uncovered, divided on the forehead in black, glossy bandeaux, and twisted up behind. The eyes and brow are noble, and the nose is of a somewhat Jewish character; the chin a little recedes, and the mouth is not good, though mobile, flashing out a sudden smile with its white projecting teeth. There is not sweetness in the face, but great moral as well as intellectual capacities–only it never *could* have been a beautiful face, which a good deal surprised me. The chief difference in it since it was younger is probably that the cheeks are considerably fuller than they used to be, but this of course does not alter the type. Her complexion is of a deep olive. I observed that her hands were small and well-shaped. We sate with her perhaps three-quarters of an hour or more—in which time she gave advice and various directions to two or three young men who were there, showing her confidence in us by the freest use of names and allusions of facts.

This "confidence" may have been, of course, a lack of consideration for her guests. Elizabeth noted Sand's trait of leadership, which Elizabeth called "masculine," as she had identified this quality in the sonnets on Sand.

She seemed to be, in fact, *the man* in that company, and the profound respect with which she was listened to a good deal impressed me. You are aware from the newspapers that she came to Paris for the purpose of seeing the President in behalf of certain of her friends, and that it was a successful mediation. What is peculiar in her manners and conversation is the absolute simplicity of both. Her voice is low and rapid, without emphasis or variety of modulation. Except one brilliant smile, she was grave—indeed, she was speaking of grave matters, and many of her friends are in adversity. But you could not help seeing (both Robert and I saw it) that in all she said, even in her kindness and pity, there was an under-current of scorn. A scorn of pleasing she evidently had; there never could have been a colour of coquetry in that woman. Her very freedom from affectation and consciousness had a touch of disdain.

The "undercurrent of scorn" was no doubt Sand's ennui with much of what was taking place around her, especially visits from Englishmen, but Elizabeth was determined to admire her and overlooked any lack of genuine warmth. Before she left she opened the door to another visit by putting Sand in a position of having to invite them again, but Sand made no overture that was not promoted by Elizabeth:

But I liked her. I did not love her, but I felt the burning soul through all that quietness, and was not disappointed in George Sand. When we rose to go I could not help saying, 'C'est pour la derniere fois,' and then she asked us to repeat our visit next Sunday and excused herself from coming to see us on the ground of a great press of engagements. She kissed me again when we went away, and Robert kissed her hand.

She concluded the letter with a statement of regret:

Lady Elgin has offered to take him one day this week to visit Lamartine (who, we hear, will be glad to see us, having a cordial feeling towards England and English poets), but I shall wait for some very warm day for that visit, not meaning to run mortal risks, except for George Sand. *Nota bene.* We didn't see her smoke.[13]

Although Robert had the experience, seeing Sand smoke was one ambition of Elizabeth's which was never satisfied.

The second visit to Sand is recorded in Elizabeth's letter to her friend, Mrs. Jameson.

And now, am I to tell you that I have seen George Sand twice, and am to see her again? Ah, there is not time to tell you, for I must shut up this letter. She sate, like a priestess, the other morning in a circle of eight or nine men, giving no oracles, except with her splendid eyes, sitting at the corner of the fire, and warming her feet quietly, in general silence of the most profound deference. There was something in the calm disdain of it which pleased me, and struck me as characteristic. She was George Sand, that was enough: you wanted no proof of it. Robert observed that 'if any other mistress of a house had behaved so, he would have walked out of the room'—but, as it was, no sort of incivility was meant. In fact, we hear that she 'likes us very much,' and as we went away she called me 'chere Madame' and kissed me, and desired to see us both again.[14]

But Elizabeth's sister Arabella was more adept at reading between the lines and thought that Sand was not nearly so receptive as she should have been to two visiting British celebrities who had such appreciation of her. Elizabeth of course refused to accept this interpretation of Sand's behavior and in writing her brother George protested Arabella's conclusion.

We have not yet seen Lamartine (but shall)—nor have we seen George Sand yet for the third time–Tell Arabel she is far too severe on her indeed–There was not the least intention on her part of being otherwise than most cordial to us—& the confidence she showed us was fuller of compliment than any banality of mere manner could be—The effects were singular notwithstanding—you should have seen the disdain with which she looked at my respirator—I took it out of my muff to show it to her—because her chest is not strong, & though better since she came to Paris, she has had a great deal of cough & was bled for this the other day—"Oh"—said she "life wouldn't be worth the trouble of such precautions"—And when somebody enquired how she was—"Je ne me porte pas bien," she answered —"but as to that, I never think of it except when I'm asked"— which perhaps was a way of saying "Dont ask." She nevertheless looked very well that day—Brilliant eyes, certainly, & a smile which outflashed them—only so rare a smile.[15]

Later, however, in a letter to her sister Henrietta, Elizabeth offered evidence that Sand was interested in her English friends:

Oh Henrietta—you will never guess what I am going to do tonight. I am going (by invitation) with Robert to see the first representation of George Sand's new play at the Gymnase. She wrote me the kindest note possible three days since—here's a part of it which I shall write out for Arabel, because Arabel thinks she isn't kind.[16]

Then follow six lines in French in which Sand apologized

for not sending seats in the loge but two fauteuils; if this arrangement did not suit the Brownings she offered a loge for the second night. Elizabeth accepted, although she told Sand she had not been out of the house during the winter. She and Robert talked it over and decided if the weather was too cold, she would not offer herself a "sacrifice to idols," even to George Sand.

The following month, upon hearing a rumor that Sand was ill, Elizabeth and Robert called at her house to inquire; however, they did not get a chance to offer their sympathies. There was in fact no third visit, since Elizabeth wrote Miss Mitford on 7 April 1852 that they called on Sand a third time but did not see her. Yet Robert saw Sand without Elizabeth on perhaps four other occasions. As she relates,

> Once he met her near the Tuileries, offered her his arm, and walked with her the whole length of the gardens. She was not on that occasion looking as well as usual, being a little too much 'endimanchee' in terrestrial lavenders and supercelestial blues—not, in fact, dressed with the remarkable taste which he has seen in her at other times. Her usual costume is both pretty and quiet, and the fashionable waistcoat and jacket (which are a spectacle in all the 'Ladies' Companions' of the day) make the only approach to masculine *wearings* to be observed in her. She has great nicety and refinement in her personal ways, I think, and the cigarette is really a feminine weapon if properly understood. Ah, but I didn't see her smoke. I was unfortunate. I could only go with Robert three times to her house, and once she was out. He was really very good and kind to let me go at all, after he found the sort of society rampant around her. He didn't like it extremely, but being the prince of husbands, he was lenient to my desires and yielded the point. She seems to live in the abomination of desolation, as far as regards society

—crowds of ill-bred men who adore her *à genoux bas,* betwixt a puff of smoke and an ejection of saliva. Society of the ragged Red diluted with the lower theatrical. She herself so different, so apart, as alone in her melancholy disdain. I was deeply interested in that poor woman, I felt a profound compassion for her. I did not mind much the Greek in Greek costume who tutoyed her, and kissed her, I believe, so Robert said; or the other vulgar man of the theatre who went down on his knees and called her 'sublime.' 'Caprice d'amitié,' said she, with her quiet, gentle scorn. A noble woman, under the mud, be certain. *I* would kneel down to her too, if she would leave it all, throw it off, and be herself as God made her. Perhaps she doesn't care for anybody by this time—who knows? She wrote one, or two, or three kind notes to me, and promised to 'venir m'embrasser' before she left Paris; but she did not come. We both tried hard to please her, and she told a friend of ours that she 'liked us;' only we always felt that we couldn't penetrate—couldn't really *touch* her—it was all in vain. Her play failed, though full of talent. It didn't draw, and was withdrawn accordingly. I wish she would keep to her romances, in which her real power lies.[17]

Robert even more than Elizabeth knew that Sand was not really interested in them, complaining that he could not get on with her; as soon as the ice was broken a new frost came between them.[18] And Sand returned none of their calls in spite of Elizabeth's urgings.

Keeping up with French writers, always being sure that Miss Mitford was informed, Elizabeth wrote that Alfred Musset had real poetic qualities rather than great powers, and she added revealingly that his latest love was the French actress who once captured young Matthew Arnold's imagination—Rachel. Elizabeth noted that Rachel was third among Musset's mistresses: "He began with the Princess Belgiojoso—followed George Sand—Rachel finishes, and is likely to 'finish' in every sense. In the intervals, he plays at chess. There's the anatomy of a *man*."[19]

Writing to Mrs. Jameson that same month, Elizabeth told of her visit to the theater to see Dumas's *La Dame aux camélias,* then complained that she had not been to the theater since, being unable to go to see Sand's *Les Vacances de Pandolphe* even though Sand had sent them tickets for the first night. Apparently this is the play about which Elizabeth had written to Henrietta the previous month. Elizabeth regretted the failure of her heroine's play and related her heroine's departure from Paris, adding that she was likely to return soon.

Elizabeth defended Sand against the charge that she was a bad republican because she had made peace with Louis Napoleon. Both Sand and Napoleon were her idols, and she defended both, saying that it was only on behalf of her Red friends that Sand had gone to see Napoleon and that she had used his friendship to aid her friends who were in distress. Later that summer she again defended Sand, this time against a minor charge—Miss Mitford had compared Sand with Mary Anne Browne, whom Miss Mitford thought approached Sand in the "passion" of her works. Elizabeth stated bluntly that she did not always agree with her friend and said that the poems Miss Mitford quoted would not bear her out "even one fiftieth degree in such an opinion."[20]

Elizabeth's high opinion of Sand as a literary genius never wavered regardless of Sand's personal indifference to the Brownings. A joint letter from Elizabeth and Robert to Mrs. Jameson in December 1855 commented enthusiastically on their reading the *Histoire de ma Vie.*

Oh! George Sand. How magnificent that eighteenth volume is; I mean the volume which concludes with the views upon the sexes! After all, and through all, if her hands are ever so defiled, that woman has a clean soul.

On the magnetic subjects, too, her 'je ne sais' is worthy of her. And yet, more is to be known, I am sure, than she knows.

I read this book so eagerly and earnestly that I seem to burn it up before me. Really there are great things in it.

And to hear people talking it over coldly, pulling it leaf from leaf!

Robert quite joins with me at last. He is intensely interested, and full of admiration.[21]

And two letters to Henrietta, nearly at the same time as the letter to Mrs. Jameson, tell of the Brownings reading Sand's memoirs. In November Elizabeth complained surprisingly that even Sand "is dull on purpose to vex me," but the next month the period of ennui had passed: "We do nothing but smoulder over the fire and read George Sand's memoirs—which disappoint everybody (except me) because they are not wicked as was expected."[22]

By May 1856 Elizabeth had lost none of her continuing fascination with Sand. A letter from Paris to Mrs. Jameson told of her socializing and mentioned two perennial heroes—Sand and Cavour.

To-night he [Robert] is going to Madame Mohl, who is well and as vivacious as ever. When Monckton Milnes was in Paris he dined with him in company with Mignet, Cavour, George Sand, and an empty chair in which Lamartine was expected to sit. George Sand had an ivy wreath round her head, and looked like herself. But Lady Monson will talk to you of *her,* better than I can. Now, mind you ask Lady Monson.[23]

This letter was written in the same year as the publication of Elizabeth's blank verse romance, *Aurora Leigh,* in which the rights of women were as strongly supported as they were by any English woman writing in the mid-Victorian period.[24] The book, Elizabeth's best-selling volume, naturally got a mixed reception in England. Swinburne praised it; so did Ruskin and many of the Pre-Raphaelite group. But to many readers the book was shameless. The *Dublin University Magazine* stated that although written by a woman, the book should be a "closed volume for her own sex." George Barrett, Elizabeth's brother, told Arabella it was a worse book than *Don Juan,* which Papa kept locked in a drawer; a number of elderly women complained that they never felt pure after reading it; and anxious mothers kept it away from their daughters.[25] It was a book worthy of a devotee of George Sand, and it is no coincidence that Elizabeth selected Sand's Christian name as the name for her heroine.

Although Sand to Robert was probably never more than an occasional interest that he shared with his wife, he did go so far as to use Sand as a model for a character in a poem, "Respectability," published in *Men and Women* (1855).[26] There Robert describes two bohemian lovers strolling at night, when they see lights flare at the Institute, a place where respectable people congregate and where Guizot and Montalembert can go through a ceremony together even though they hate each other. One of the lovers speaks:

> I know! The world proscribes not love;
> Allows my finger to caress
> Your lips' contour and downiness,

> Provided it supply a glove.
> The world's good word! the Institute!
> Guizot receives Montalembert!
> Eh? Down the court three lampions flare:
> Put forward your best foot! (ll. 17–24)

The world or society steeped in present day convention will accept conventional hatred much more readily than it will accept unconventional love. With little justice, therefore, the world has not

> Designed to proclaim, "I know you both,
> Have recognized your plighted troth,
> Am sponsor for you; live in peace." (ll. 1–4)

"Respectability" is sympathetic to the attitudes that Sand and Elizabeth shared on convention, love and hate, and the relation of the sexes. There are no direct references to Sand in Browning's works after Elizabeth's death in 1861.

It would be difficult to exaggerate Elizabeth's admiration for George Sand or to emphasize too much what Sand meant to her during her long years of illness. Sand furnished inspiration, both for action in Elizabeth's own life and for at least one major work. Elizabeth Barrett Browning, like George Eliot, Charlotte Brontë, Jane Carlyle, and other emancipated English women of the day, found an affinity with the French authoress. Sand achieved a freedom in her personal life that they aspired to, and for that reason she was both symbol and inspiration.

VII

George Eliot and George Sand

The ultimatum of human wisdom on human sorrow.
George Eliot, *Letters*

Still another participant in the cult of George Sand was George Eliot, who like Arnold found inspiration in Sand's *vie idéale.* When J. W. Cross wrote the biography of his wife, Mary Ann Evans, later famous under the pen name George Eliot, he surveyed the literary scene at the time of her birth in 1819: Jane Austen had published her last novel eighteen months before; Dickens and Thackeray were both boys at school; Scott's *Waverley* series was six years old; and George Sand, then nineteen, was leaving the Berry countryside for the Couvent des Anglaises in Paris.[1] Cross's linking of Sand to Eliot and other English novelists is not surprising, for Eliot by her own admission owed a considerable debt to Sand; furthermore there are facets in the personalities of the two women that are quite similar.

Both Sand and Eliot were born in small rural towns, and some of their most successful works have settings in these areas, the province of Berry in Sand's writings and Warwickshire in Eliot's. Each was compelled early in life to become self-sufficient: the death of Sand's father thrust her toward maturity; Eliot's beginning independence came at the age of five when she was put in a private boarding school because of her mother's ill health. Both were steeped in the melancholia of the age. The inscription to evening that Sand wrote in her youth at Nohant is matched by the solemn musings of Eliot's first published poem, in which a young girl walks alone through the fields at evening, bidding farewell to the books, fields, and people she has loved. The poem had a biblical inscription that was a forcible reminder of the transiency of this life: "Knowing that shortly I must put off this my tabernacle."[2]

Both Sand and Eliot were intensely religious when they were young. Sand had considered taking the veil, and Eliot's youthful actions were guided by an evangelical zeal, when her favorite author was Hannah More and when she often upbraided her brother Isaac for his High Church views. Both Sand and Eliot subsequently went through a period of disturbing religious doubt. Sand's conversion to orthodoxy lasted only a short time, while she was at the Couvent des Anglaises. Her attitude toward the Roman Catholic Church, in the main, was influenced by the teaching of her grandmother, who had read widely in the eighteenth-century philosophes and had passed on her skepticism to her granddaughter. Eliot's loss of faith was brought on by many things: Isaac Taylor's *Ancient Christianity and Oxford Tracts,* which she read as an antidote to the doctrines of Oxford High Churchmen, contained facts that preyed on her mind about the early church fathers. The "Coventry intellectuals"—the Brays and the Hennells—also played their part in destroying Eliot's faith in religious orthodoxy: through them she became acquainted with Strauss's *Leben Jesu* and other works of higher criticism that destroyed her faith in the

Bible as the revealed word.[3] Yet neither Sand nor Eliot ever completely abandoned the influence of religious training. Sand's skepticism made her doubt the Catholic faith that Chateaubriand defended; yet she could never put aside religion. The result was her sympathy with Protestantism. Likewise, although skeptical of orthodoxy, Eliot became a champion of the good effects of orthodoxy.

Both Sand and Eliot were interested in social reform: Eliot's *Felix Holt* may be called a godson of Sand's *Le Meunier d'Angibault;* each deals with the working classes and urges their improvement.

Music meant a great deal to both writers. Sand's total portrait must include her deep love of music, which explains in part her friendship with Liszt and her relationship with Chopin. Eliot heard Liszt play when she was in Europe, and she was reminded of both Liszt and Sand; she wrote to Charles Bray:

> Liszt is the first really inspired man I ever saw. His face might serve as a model for a St. John in its sweetness when he is in repose but seated at the piano he is as grand as one of Michael Angelo's prophets. When I read George Sand's letter to Franz Liszt, in her 'Lettres d'un voyageur,' I little thought that I should ever be seated tete-a-tete with him for an hour, as I was yesterday and telling him my ideas and feelings.[4]

The most striking similarity between Sand and Eliot is the strong streak of masculine independence in their personalities that made each seek fulfillment in her own way, Sand's path leading to promiscuity in love affairs, Eliot's to a common-law marriage with George Henry Lewes. In Eliot's relationship with Lewes, as in Sand's with Chopin (or as in Sand's relationship with any of her lovers), the woman was the stronger and more prominent in the eyes of the world.

Eliot and Lewes's love affair is a fascinating chapter in Victorian literary history. Lewes was often accused of holding bohemian views, and he could not win a divorce from his wife because he had condoned her adultery. Yet the Eliot and Lewes relationship eventually won the respect of many prominent Victorians, including Carlyle, Tennyson, and Browning, who often called to pay their respects at the Priory, where the couple settled in the seventh year of their common-law marriage. The salon that George Eliot held there for the prominent Victorians, usually male, is reminiscent of the literary gatherings Sand held for admirers in Paris and at Nohant. Ironically enough, Eliot's marriage to J. W. Cross shortly after Lewes's death shocked people who had uneasily accepted her relationship with Lewes. Like Sand, the English George possessed all her life the ability to set tongues to wagging.[5]

Although some of these comparisons may seem tenuous, it is impossible to overlook the tremendous influence which Eliot, in her letters, admits that Sand exerted on her, the greatest influence coming at a time when Eliot was undergoing her soul crisis.

Sometimes Eliot's reference to Sand was merely a comparison of herself to characters in Sand's works, showing how familiar she was with them. In a letter dated December 1845 to her friend Sara Hennell she referred to proofs she had received for the translation she was doing of Strauss's *Leben Jesu*. Eliot commented: "I am writing to tell you how vexed I am to see the indistinctness of the Greek in the proof. It makes my eyes ache to look at it. . . . One has need be Alexis [the learned monk in *Spiridion*] to read it." Nearly three years later, again in a letter to Sara Hennell, Eliot drew on the same book for a comparison of her affection for Sara: "You are ever with me as Spiridion was with Alexis and Angel." A similar reference to one of Sand's works occurred in another letter, again to Sara Hennell, written in 1849: "Think of Babylon being unearthed in spite of the prophecies! Truly we are looking before and after au jour d'aujourd'hui, as Monsieur Bricolin [a nouveau riche peasant in *Le Meunier d'Angibault*] says."[6]

The novels by Sand that Eliot apparently admired most were the *Lettres d'un Voyageur* and *Lélia*. Unlike Elizabeth Barrett Browning, Eliot found a great deal to admire in the latter. In 1847, for instance, she wrote to Sara Hennell: "How are you, meine Geliebte, and how do you like Lelia, of which you have never spoken one word. . . . I am provoked with you for being in the least pleased with Disraeli's Tancred, but if you have found out any lofty meaning in it or any true picturing of life, tell it me and I will recant."[7] If Disraeli had little to offer Eliot, Sand had much. Eliot wrote of the *Lettres* and of *Lélia* this comment which shows as well her high regard for Miss Hennell's reactions to books they read:

> I am reading George Sand's "Lettres d'un Voyageur" with great delight, and hoping that they will some time do you as much good as they do me. In the meantime I think the short letter about "Lelia" will interest you. It has a very deep meaning to my apprehension. You can send back the pages when you have

duly digested them. I once said of you that yours was a sort of alkali nature, which would detect the slightest acid of falsehood. You began to phiz-zz directly it approached you. I want you as a test.[8]

In the same letter she made this comment about love:

I now begin to see the necessity of the arrangement (a bad word) that love should determine people's fate while they are young. It is so impossible to admire—*'s'enthousiasmer'* of—an individual as one gets older.

These sentiments were written in 1848, six years before Eliot became Lewes's common-law wife. How much Sand influenced Eliot in her attitudes toward love and marriage, one can only speculate. Moraud, however, states that Eliot would not have entered into life with Lewes without Sand's example. This may be an extreme position, similar to Moraud's statement that Sand furnished Eliot "intellectual food" to replace Orthodoxy, when Eliot renounced her religion.[9] But the latter position is easier to defend by Eliot's letters. In 1849 Eliot wrote John Sibree, quoting Sand to express the despair she felt as her evangelical faith failed to support her:

Well I will send you a stanza I picked up the other day in George Sand's Lettres d'un Voyageur, which is almost the ultimatum of human wisdom on the question of human sorrow. It will either make you laugh or weep ("iron tears" of course) and so it must do good.

Le bonheur et le malheur
Nous viennent du même auteur
Voilà la *ressemblance.*
Le bonheur nous rend heureux,
Et le malheur malheureux,
Voilà la différence.

Ah! here comes a cup of coffee to console me. When I have taken it I will tell you what G.S. says. "Sais-tu bien que tout est dit devant Dieu et devant les hommes quand l'homme infortune demande compte de ses maux et qu'il obtienne cette response? Qu'y a-t-il de plus? Rien."[10]

Other references exist which also indicate that Sand was as much an idol to Eliot as she was to Elizabeth Browning, although Eliot was never quite so extravagant in her praise. She wrote jointly to the Brays and the Hennells in 1848, "Dear Cara, your husband desired me to send you the newspaper paragraph about George Sand, and I obey —but if you disapprove, utter none of your blasphemies to me." Again, writing to Sara Hennell, Eliot asked for criticism of *Jacques* but warned against "too many blasphemies against my divinity."[11]

In another letter to Sara Hennell in February 1849, Eliot gave a careful analysis of what writers like Rousseau and Sand meant to her:

I wish you thoroughly to understand that the writers who have most profoundly influenced me—who have rolled away the waters from their bed raised new mountains and spread delicious valleys for me—are not in the least oracles to me. It is just possible that I may not embrace one of their opinions, that I may wish my life to be shaped quite differently from theirs. For instance it would signify nothing to me if a very wise person were to stun me with proofs that Rousseau's view of life, religion, and government are miserably erroneous—that he was guilty of some of the worst bassesses that have degraded civilized man. I might admit all this—and it would be not the less true that Rousseau's genius has sent that electric thrill through my intellectual and moral frame which has awakened me to new perceptions, which has made man and nature a fresh world of thought and feeling to me—and this not by teaching me any new belief. It is simply that the rushing mighty wind of his inspiration has so quickened my faculties that I have been able to shape more definitely for myself ideas which had previously dwelt as dim 'ahnungen' in my soul—the fire of his genius has so fused together old thoughts and prejudices that I have been ready to make new combinations.

It is thus with G. Sand. I should never dream of going to her writings as a moral code or text-book. I don't care whether I agree with her about marriage or not—whether I think the design of her plot correct or that she had no precise design at all but began to write as the spirit moved her and trusted to Providence for the catastrophe, which I think the more probable case—it is sufficient for me as a reason for bowing before her in eternal gratitude to the 'great power of God' manifested in her—that I cannot read six pages of hers without feeling that it is given to her to delineate human passion and its results—(and I must say in spite of your judgment) some of the moral instincts and their tendencies—with such truthfulness such nicety of discrimination such tragic power and withal such loving gentle humour that one might live a century with nothing but one's own dull faculties and not know so much as those six pages will suggest.[12]

It is interesting to note that Eliot's insight into Sand's approach to her art is sounder than Lewes's opinion stated in an article published in *Foreign Quarterly* in 1844 in which he contended that Sand often revised what she wrote, constructing her plots with great care.

Eliot may have had some Anglo-Saxon reservations about Sand's extreme views on marriage, that it was a cancer of society. Still, her praise of *Jacques* which shocked many Victorians—such as the critic writing in the *Foreign and Colonial Review* in 1843 and A. Innes Shand writing in *Blackwood's* in 1877—may be taken as evidence of Sand's influence on her in the unconventional step she finally took with Lewes. In the same letter to Sara Hennell, Eliot said about *Jacques:*

> The psychological anatomy of Jacques Fernande in the early days of their marriage seems quite preternaturally true—I mean that her power of describing it is preternatural. Fernande and Jacques are merely the masculine and the feminine nature and their early married life an everyday tragedy—but I will not dilate on the book or on your criticism for I am so sleepy that I should write nothing but betises.

Eliot probably had in mind the statement in which Jacques calls marriage "one of the most barbarous institutions that society has debauched."[13]

Both Eliot and Lewes, interestingly enough, were outspoken advocates of Sand years before they met. Lewes's first major review of Sand's works was in 1844; Eliot's first reference to Sand in her letters was in 1845 to Sara Hennell. She may have discovered Sand through the Brays, or her discovery may have been the result of her own intellectual curiosity. The remark by her father—about all the "rigamorole" of the "frog-eaters," who could put nothing but nonsense in his daughter's head—establishes that Eliot was reading French novels at least by the early 1840s. She and Lewes met after she became assistant editor to John Chapman of the *Westminster Review* in 1851, and in 1854 she and Lewes formed the liaison that seemed an imitation of Sand's characters. Admiration for Sand, Rousseau, Comte, and French liberal politics were views the two held in common, and their sympathy for Sand no doubt encouraged them in their final decision. Eliot's liberal views in politics were expressed, for example, shortly after the Revolution of 1848, when she wrote of her admiration of the French working class, whom she thought more sensitive to social problems than the English masses.[14]

By 1850 Sand's subject matter had so changed in her pastoral novels that Eliot wrote her friends Mr. and Mrs. Bray from Geneva: "You know that George Sand writes for the theatre? Her Francois le Champi, une comedie, is simplicity and purity itself. The seven devils are cast out."[15] Eliot's comment is paralleled by the amelioration of attitudes toward Sand in British periodicals at that time.

In 1852, now on the staff of the *Westminster Review,* Eliot wrote the Brays from London about Thackeray's *Henry Esmond,* which she called "the most uncomfortable book you can imagine." Then she reminded Mrs. Bray of her displeasure with Sand's *François le Champi* and makes the comment: "Well, the story of Esmond is just the same. The hero is in love with the daughter all through the book, and marries the mother at the end." That same year she wrote to Sara Hennell that she had been hearing Pierre Leroux, who had escaped to England after the coup d'etat of 1851, and she identified him as Sand's friend. Again in 1852, to the Brays and Sara Hennell, Eliot wrote: "I am ashamed to teaze you so—but I must beg you to send me Geo. Sand's works (tomorrow or Friday if possible) and also I shall be grateful if you will lend me—what I think you have—an English edition of *Corinne* and Miss Austen's 'Sense and Sensibility.' "[16]

The next year, in writing to the Brays for an opinion of Charlotte Brontë's *Villette,* Eliot compared Brontë favorably with Sand. And when Eliot was having trouble getting the right translation for *Mill on the Floss,* she wrote from London to her translator, François d'Albert-Durade:

I can well imagine that you find 'The Mill' more difficult to render than 'Adam.' But would it be inadmissible to represent in French, at least in some degree, those "intermediaires entre le style commun et le style elegant" to which you refer? It seems to me that I have discerned such shades very strikingly rendered in Balzac, and occasionally in George Sand. Balzac, I think, dares to be thoroughly colloquial, in spite of French strait-lacing. Even in English this daring is far from being general. The writers who dare to be thoroughly familiar are Shakespeare, Fielding, Scott.

Later, when plans were underway to translate *Scenes of Clerical Life* into French, Eliot wrote from Florence to John Blackwood to suggest a Mrs. Blackwell, probably Anna Blackwell who had translated Sand's *Jacques* in 1847.[17]

Eliot and Lewes considered their arrangement a marriage, feeling no doubt (as had William Fox, George Sand, and many others) that the society which caused their situation had little right to judge. Still, Eliot did conduct herself with decorum; thus it has been pointed out that had she cared to make visits and to cut a swathe in London society she might have been received as "a combination of loose woman and genius—an English George Sand." But for her part she lived conservatively, generally receiving only those who mattered to her and to Lewes—Charles Dickens, Anthony Trollope, Wilkie Collins, Herbert Spencer, and Thomas Carlyle. What shocked some people, Jane Carlyle in particular, was that Eliot set herself up as a moralist.[18]

While resemblances between the lives of the two Georges can be established and Sand's influence on Eliot can be documented from Eliot's letters, it is also true that in Eliot's own day her contemporaries thought of her and Sand together. For example there is a record of a visit to the Leweses made by Charles Eliot Norton in January 1869. Norton had met Lewes at Oxford the previous summer; and as soon as he came to London, Norton says, Lewes invited him to call,

To come and see his wife, saying that she never made calls herself, but was always at home on Sunday afternoons. She is an object of great interest and great curiosity to society here. She is not received in general society, and the women who visit her are either so emancipee as not to mind what the world says about them, or have no social position to maintain. Lewes dines out a good deal, and some of the men with whom he dines go without their wives to his house on Sundays. No one whom I have heard speak, speaks in other than terms of respect of Mrs. Lewes, but the common feeling is that it will not do for society to condone so flagrant a breach as hers of a convention and a sentiment (to use no stronger terms) on which morality greatly relies for support. I suspect society is right in this.[19]

Norton described Lewes, praising him for his knowledge "in Darwin's and Lyell's departments" but stated that Lewes had the "vanity of a Frenchman"; and his moral perceptions were deemed "not acute." Norton described the luncheon, set in Lewes's study, "a cheerful room like the others, lined with well-filled bookshelves, save over the fire-place where hung a staring likeness and odious, vulgarizing portrait of Mrs. Lewes." Norton then drew this comparison:

The portrait of Mrs. Lewes reminded me, not by its own merit, of Couture's drawing of George Sand,—and there is a strong likeness to this drawing in her own face. The head and face are hardly as noble as George Sand's, but the lines are almost as strong and masculine; the cheeks are almost as heavy, and the hair is dressed in a similar style, but the eyes are not so deep, and there is less suggestion of possible beauty and possible sensuality in the general contour and in the expression. Indeed one rarely sees a plainer woman; dull complexion, dull eye, heavy features. For the greater part of two or three hours she and I talked together with little intermission. Her talk was by no means brilliant. She said not one memorable thing, but it was the talk of a person of strong mind who had thought much and felt deeply and consequently it was more than commonly interesting . . . nor is her manner perfectly simple. It is a little that, or it suggests that, of a woman who feels herself to be of mark and is accustomed, as she is, to the adoring flattery of a coterie of not undistinguished admirers.[20]

The description is also reminiscent of Elizabeth Browning's detailed account of George Sand holding court for her admirers. Another interesting parallel between Eliot and Sand is that neither was a brilliant conversationalist. The Brownings noted this fact about Sand, and Balzac observed that she had a "stupid look" when she was thoughtful.[21]

Other writers thought of Sand and Eliot together. John Fiske wrote in November 1873 in response to an inquiry from his wife:

Well, what do I think of her? She is not a "fright" by any means. She is a plain-looking woman, but I think not especially homely. I see no reason why her photograph should not be circulated about. She is *much* better looking than George Sand. She isn't a blooming beauty, of course; you don't expect that at fifty-two; but her features are regular, her nose is very good, her eyes are a rich blue and very expressive, her mouth is very large, but it is pleasant in expression. . . . I never saw such a woman. There is nothing a bit masculine about her; she is thoroughly feminine and looks and acts as if she were made for nothing but to mother babies. But she has a power of *stating* an argument equal to any man; equal to any man do I say? I have never seen any man, except Herbert Spencer, who could state a case equal to her.[22]

And Sand and Eliot remained associated in the thoughts of critics at other times. As John Morley wrote to Sidney Colvin, who was to review *Deronda* for the *Fortnightly:* "Say what you like about George Sand. You will naturally spare George Eliot's feelings as much as critical honesty will permit."[23]

Margaret Oliphant was an early critic to draw literary comparisons between Sand and Eliot. Writing for *Blackwood's* in 1874, in a review entitled "Two Cities—Two Books," Mrs. Oliphant linked Eliot's *Romola* and Sand's *Consuelo.* While reminiscing about the settings of those two books, Florence and Venice, she remarked that Eliot's novel was actually sold as a guidebook for Florence; she thought likewise that Sand's vivid descriptions would evoke memories of Venice from people who had been there. She then commented on the irony that these two great cities should be reduced to relying on tourists and novelists to keep their fame alive. Although Mrs. Oliphant related a great deal about the plot of each novel, the chief comparison she drew was that each novel concerned an unfortunate love affair. She found Sand's heroine superior to all around her but unaware of her superiority; Eliot's heroine, she commented, was superior to all around her and knew that she was superior. Sand fared a little better than Eliot in this review, for Mrs. Oliphant described Sand's heroine as more "real, natural, simple, and true."

An unidentified reviewer in the *Temple Bar* in 1885 ended an article on Sand by comparing her to Eliot, calling them the "two great female novelists of the century" and praising both for their democratic leanings. The reviewer commented on the strange coincidence that both writers made the same statement, one after hearing Liszt play, the other after hearing Mendelssohn: "Had I any genius, *that* is the form I should have wished to take, for then I could have spoken to all my fellow men." The reviewer described Eliot as less passionate than Sand, who "lost the right road and wandered in the desert." Sand was weaker in "perfection of construction and finish" than Eliot, but Sand seemed stronger in delineation of female characters and in the painting of human love. The reviewer quoted Eliot on Sand: "for eloquence and depth of feeling no man approaches George Sand."[24]

Leslie Stephen also drew comparisons between the two novelists. First he gave evidence of Eliot's admiration for the French, commenting on her sympathy for Louis Blanc and for the French revolt of 1848; then he quoted the passage concerning the "electric thrill" Eliot said she got from Rousseau's works. He noticed too the passage in which Eliot described Sand as a superior "delineator of human passion." Admitting that Eliot had a retentive memory for French novels read in her youth, Stephen sidestepped an "expanded criticism" but commented that in comparing Eliot with French writers "much would have to be said of George Sand." He very perceptively pointed out that Sand's novels were "poured forth . . . with amazing spontaneity and felicity," while each of Eliot's novels was "the product of a kind of spiritual agony." In another comment on Eliot and Sand, Stephen praised Eliot's objective view of country life and preferred it over Sand's lush description, which he called "the country idyll of the sentimentalist which charms us . . . but in which our enjoyment is checked by the inevitable sense of unreality."[25]

Yet a more exhaustive comparison of the two writers exists in Marcel Moraud's *Le Romantisme français en Angleterre*. In a chapter on George Sand and Victorian England, Moraud sees Sand's influence as bearing chiefly on George Eliot; he has but brief references to her influence on Elizabeth Browning and hardly mentions Matthew Arnold's visit to Nohant.

Moraud thinks that Sand influenced Eliot chiefly because Sand's skepticism aided Eliot in thinking about art, life, and human destiny. Sand's life was like the "flight of the bird toward the mysterious regions; no one, except Vigny, better understood human tragedy and expressed that understanding and the human fate to wait, suffer, doubt; then the tomb opens to receive the fatigued traveller." Moraud sees also that part of the attraction Sand had for Eliot was simply her expression of revolt, and he points to Eliot's early rebellion against all restrictions, especially those placed on her because she was a woman; he quotes one of Eliot's letters to Miss Hennell expressing her truthful suffering because she had the "strength of genius of a man."[26]

To strengthen his argument Moraud might have quoted Eliot's praise for another feminist of the period, Jessie Meriton White. When Miss White was refused admission to fourteen different hospitals in England as a medical student, she became a correspondent for the *Daily News* in

Genoa. There she nursed the wounded and married a Garibaldian officer. Returning to England flaunting "a particularly evil-smelling cigar like George Sand," she won the praise of one of George Eliot's friends, who wrote the daily press a letter in praise of Miss White and her independent spirit. Eliot subsequently wrote her friend that she wished the letter had been "in large print."[27]

Moraud writes that Sand's literary influence may be traced from such things as the prominence Eliot gives to soul crises, her tendency to extend the limits of the novel, and in the role she gives to the problem of love and marriage; but unfortunately he gives scant documentation to these general points. However, when he does refer specifically to one of Eliot's novels, *Mill on the Floss,* he compares it to works by Sand and Rousseau. The farewell ride in a boat on the Floss, he says, is straight out of the *Nouvelle Héloïse.* According to Moraud, Eliot ends the novel —in this case with the death of the heroine, Maggie—in a manner unlike Sand's denouements because the British public would not accept Sand's philosophy in such matters. He agrees with George Saintsbury that Eliot is an advocate of strict union between love and marriage, an attitude that Moraud attributes to Sand's influence. The final point Moraud makes about Eliot is that she was not a profound thinker, rather she echoed conceptions she found in others—exactly Joseph Mazzini's final estimate of Sand.

As for Eliot's reception in France, Moraud points to recognition, by 1860, by such French critics as Scherer, Montégut, and Brunetière as an English writer who had "planted the flag of naturalism in England," a naturalism, "vivified by an interior principle (sympathy) which French naturalism lacked."[28] But Eliot never enjoyed the wide popular following in France that Sand enjoyed in England.[29]

There is no question that people on both sides of the Channel thought of these two foremost writers of the day in terms of comparison. Although Sand may have given little thought to Eliot, it is evident that Sand was often in Eliot's thoughts.

VIII

Matthew Arnold and George Sand

The large utterance of the early gods.
Matthew Arnold, "George Sand"

Many of the outspoken admirers of Sand in Victorian England were women: Elizabeth Barrett Browning, George Eliot, Charlotte Brontë, Geraldine Jewsbury, and Jane Carlyle—each of whom created an image of Sand that served her own need. Male Victorians, on the other hand, such as Mill, Ruskin, Dickens, Browning, and Thackeray, usually admired Sand casually. Perhaps her greatest admirer among male writers was George Henry Lewes, whose life ended in the shadow of a strong woman whose fame far surpassed his own. Yet Sand had one other champion among Victorian men writers—Matthew Arnold.

Arnold was only ten years old when *Indiana* was published in France. By the time he went to Oxford, Sand was still a controversial figure, but for most readers "her seven devils had been cast out" (to use George Eliot's phrase describing Sand's later works). By the time Arnold had decided that his age was not hospitable to poetry, Sand was well accepted, except by the *Quarterly* and a few other outposts of extreme conservatism. And when Balzac came on the scene with his so-called objective view of man, many readers, including Arnold, were so repelled that they found renewed inspiration in Sand's view of the *vie idéale.* Indeed by 1870 the image of Sand as a grandmother and the good lady of Nohant had almost completely obliterated the memory of the dangerous Saint-Simonian of the 1830s and 1840s. Arnold's published writings on Sand appeared, therefore, when she was less in need of a defender than of an admirer to call the attention of a fickle public to her works.

The basis for Arnold's interest in Sand was laid at Rugby, where Thomas Arnold, his headmaster father, stressed modern foreign languages and literatures. In a letter to his mother in 1869, Arnold wrote of his father: "Coleridge on Keble I have read . . . but my own feeling when I close the book is of papa's immense superiority to all the set, mainly because, owing to his historic sense, he was so wonderfully, for his nation, time, and profession, European, and thus so got himself out of the narrow medium in which, after all, his English friends lived."[1] One result of Thomas Arnold's European outlook was his son's interest in French literature, and the chief French writer of Arnold's youth was Sand, whom he read in the original in one of the numerous editions sold in England. He also kept up with Sand through the pages of the *Revue des Deux Mondes,* which he read faithfully.

At Oxford in 1842 Arnold's closest associates were his younger brother Thomas, Arthur Hugh Clough, and Theodore Walrond; each Sunday they took breakfast in Clough's rooms, where they discussed contemporary writers and politics. George Sand seemed to this group "the incarnation of a new spirit of revolt and renovation";[2] and besides, there was the appeal to these young men of being bold and even wicked in reading her. It was at this time Arnold and Clough reached the conclusion that they could not be sound critics if they knew only English literature,[3] and subsequently Arnold increased his knowledge of German and French writers. In particular he read widely in Sand, for whom he retained a great admiration for many years.

It was natural that in his youth he would find in Sand, who had stirred the Germans, Italians, and the French, a writer who would express a satisfactory criticism of life, and his letters reveal an enduring interest in her. Writing to Clough in 1845, he quoted from memory a passage from *Indiana* in which Indiana praises a religious attitude that, even if it encouraged political revolutions, represented idealism of the highest kind. And in the same letter Arnold gave two long quotations in the original French, one in which Jacques states that Fernande is under the power of conventional attitudes. Arnold never referred to scandal in Sand's private life—a point of concern to Clough, who tempered his admiration with moralistic criticism.[4]

In July 1846, two years after taking his degree at Oxford, Arnold made a sentimental pilgrimage to Nohant, to see the places Sand had described in her novels. Writing more than thirty years later about this visit, he recalled with nostalgia his trip to Berry and the river Indre of which he already had had a knowledge from *Jeanne*.[5] He tells how he got out Cassini's "great map" at the Bodleian Library, took the railway through the center of France to Vierzon; then from there went by diligences, changing each time to a humbler one at Châteauroux and La Châtre until he reached Boussac. He passed by the chateau of

Nohant, without stopping, describing it as "a plain house by the roadside, with a walled garden." But at Boussac he addressed to George Sand "the sort of letter of which she must in her lifetime have had scores, a letter conveying to her, in bad French, the homage of a youthful and enthusiastic foreigner who had read her works with delight." Sand received what Arnold calls his "infliction" good-naturedly, and sent a message by a servant from Nohant, saying she would welcome him if he chose to call.

He arrived at midday and found breakfast not yet over. Sand, as he no doubt had expected, was surrounded by a large group of admirers. Arnold admits that he entered with some trepidation but Sand's simplicity of manner put him at ease. She pointed out some of those present—Sand's two children, Maurice and Solange, whom he already knew from her books, probably *Lettres d'un Voyageur*. Chopin was there; Arnold refers to "his wonderful eyes."

Arnold was pleased to note nothing unconventional in Sand's dress. "She was not in man's clothes, she wore a sort of costume not impossible, I should think (although on these matters I speak with hesitation), to members of the fair sex at this hour amongst ourselves, as an out-door dress for the country or for Scotland." She honored him by asking him to sit by her while she poured for him "the insipid and depressing beverage for which English people are thought abroad to be always thirsting,—tea."

Arnold records that they talked, Sand commenting on the French countryside, the Berry peasants whom she had idealized in fiction, and of Switzerland, next on his itinerary. Arnold notes that she "touched politely by a few questions and remarks" upon England; he recalled her mentioning Oxford, Cambridge, Byron, and Bulwer. He found her "eyes, head, bearing, all striking," but mainly he was impressed, as were the Brownings, with Sand's "frank, cordial simplicity." After breakfast she took him into the garden, where she talked, again politely, about Arnold himself and his plans, then left him at the gate after heartily shaking hands. For Sand's impressions of Arnold, there is a record in Arnold's letters. Much later he wrote his sister "Fan": "I also heard from Morley yesterday that G. Sand had said to Renan that when she saw me years ago, *'Je lui faisais l'effet d'un Milton jeune et voyageant.'* " Renan told him this.[6]

Iris Sells, in her book on Matthew Arnold and his debt to French writers, adds embellishments concerning the visit: that Sand mentioned Imenstrom, the home of Obermann (since Arnold was going to Switzerland), Sainte-Beuve, and Maurice de Guérin, whom Sand had written about in the May 1840 issue of the *Revue des Deux Mondes,* and that Arnold inquired how he could obtain these articles. Sells also feels confident that Sand talked of the "course à Chamouni," which she had made in 1836 with Madame d'Agoult and Liszt, and which she described in *Lettres d'un Voyageur,* one of her four most representative works, according to Arnold. Sells feels sure that after Arnold left Sand, he acquired her edition of Sénancour's *Obermann,* her *Hiver à Majorque,* and perhaps some back numbers of the *Revue des Deux Mondes,* which contained Guérin's *Centaur.* That Arnold chose quotations from

Obermann, which were also favorites of Sand's, quoted in her preface to that work, makes Sells confident that Arnold had Sand's edition of *Obermann.*[7]

He went back to England from Nohant much affected, if outward appearance served as an indication. Clough commented:

> Matt is full of Parisianism; theatres in general, and Rachel in special: he enters the room with a chanson of Beranger's on his lips—for the sake of French words almost *conscious* of tune: his carriage shows him in fancy parading the rue de Rivoli;—and his hair is guiltless of English scissors: he breakfasts at twelve, and never dines in Hall, and in the week or 8 days rather (for 2 Sundays must be included) he has been to Chapel *once.*[8]

Although his interest in Sand continued, Arnold was in fact displeased by some of her political activity in 1848, when she had written two letters for the newspaper *La Vraie République* expressing disapproval of the new government's policy allowing the provinces to be controlled by the people of Paris. Arnold expressed disapproval of the letters and Sand's elaborate praise for "the people." Five years later he wrote Clough that he was growing tired of his French heroine even though he preferred her to "the woman Stowe," and in August 1853 he wrote Clough: "I am trying to re-read Valentine—but stick—except in the scenery bits."[9] These descriptive passages continued to appeal to Arnold twenty years afterward when he wrote his anniversary article on Sand for the *Fortnightly Review.*

In France again in 1859, as inspector of schools, Arnold had become friendly with Merimée, once Sand's lover, and with Sand's old confidant, Sainte-Beuve. Arnold prided himself on his French connections and liked the dignity they accorded him; as he wrote his mother, "This is my last appearance abroad as 'Monsieur le Professeur Docteur Arnold, Directeur-General de toutes les Ecoles de la Grand Bretagne,' as my French friends will have it that I am."[10] It was this letter that began speculation that Arnold may have seen Sand again that year, for he told his mother, "I go to Berri on Sunday to see George Sand." Yet he wrote his wife five days later that Sainte-Beuve advised him to go see Sand but that he was disinclined "to take so long a journey to see such a fat old Muse."[11] In the same letter Arnold wrote of taking dinner at Le Restaurant du Quartier with Sainte-Beuve, "in the cabinet where G. Sand, when she is in Paris, comes and dines every day." After dinner Sainte-Beuve took Arnold to his house and showed him letters he had received from both Sand and Musset "at the time of their love affair" and "at the time of their rupture." Arnold's reaction was one of great interest. He made no criticism of Sainte-Beuve for revealing the content of the letters; evidently anything the old Muse wrote was worthy of scrutiny. Arnold commented to his wife:

> You may imagine how interesting this was after *Elle et Lui.* I will tell you about them when we meet. Sainte-Beuve says I must read *Lui et Elle,* to finish the history, and then to complete it all, a few pages in the *Memoirs* of Mogador about Musset. As for G. Sand and him, Sainte-Beuve says '*Tout le mal* qu'ils ont dit l'un de l'autre est vrai.' But de Musset's letters were, I must say, those of a *gentleman* of the first water.[12]

Sand's death in 1876 brought forth this eulogy: "Her death has been much in my mind; she was the greatest spirit in our European world from the time that Goethe departed. With all her faults and Frenchism, she was this, I must write a few pages about her."[13] But nearly a year later the "few pages" still had not been completed, and in May 1877 he wrote his wife, "G. Sand is beginning to weigh upon me greatly, though she also interests me very much; the old feeling of liking for her and of refreshment from her, in spite of her faults, comes back."[14]

The article was published a month later in the *Fortnightly Review* and tells of Sand's impact on Arnold in his youth and analyzes his admiration for her. While it is his major writing on Sand, it does not end his numerous references to her. For instance, writing again for the *Fortnightly Review* in 1880 on "Copyright," Arnold uses Sand for an important reference; and there is occasional mention of her in his letters up to his death. Writing to his good friend Lady de Rothschild, in 1883, he spoke of the "startling event" of Gambetta's death but confesses he had "caught from G. Sand her strong dislike of Gambetta."[15]

He retained an interest in Sand until the end of his life. As late as February 1888 he wrote his elder daughter Lucy, from Cobham: "I am reading to myself the latter volumes of G. Sand's correspondence, and find them so interesting that I shall write an article on 'the old age of George Sand.' "[16] But the piece never was written before Arnold's death in April of that year.

Evidence of Sand's influence on Arnold's poetry is tenuous at best. Probably "Obermann" and "Obermann Once More" express an affinity for ideas and emotions shared by Sand, Sénancour, Sainte-Beuve, and Arnold more than they reveal a direct influence; but the two poems are important for an understanding of Arnold's admiration for Sand.

The discoverer of Sénancour was Sand's and Arnold's friend, Sainte-Beuve, who declared Sénancour the real father of French romanticism rather than Chateaubriand. When Sainte-Beuve wrote a preface for the 1833 edition of Sénancour's *Obermann,* he called the work to Sand's attention. She in turn wrote an article for the *Revue des Deux Mondes,* professing great admiration for the work. It no doubt influenced her *Lélia,* and she became known as the "sister" of Obermann, especially after Sainte-Beuve pointed out Sénancour's influence on her. She wrote an admiring preface for an 1840 edition of *Obermann,* in which she described different types of sufferers;[17] but she was later to spend a great deal of energy dissociating herself from the book to prevent her works being used to explain her private life.

Whether Arnold knew this edition of *Obermann* with Sand's preface before he wrote his two poems on the subject is debatable. Iris Sells affirms that he did.[18] Kenneth Allott, though agreeing that Sells's claim is justifiable, feels it is not to be taken as definite. It is known that when he died Arnold had among his books a copy of Sénancour's *Obermann* with Sand's preface.[19] And in an explanatory note which Arnold first published in 1868 to "Stanzas in Memory of the Author of 'Obermann,'" he sketched in four paragraphs the life of Sénancour and commented that his work has passages that "have attracted and charmed some of the most remarkable spirits of this century, such as George Sand and Sainte-Beuve, and will probably always find a certain number of spirits whom they touch and interest."[20] Arnold's note further related the qualities he listed in his anniversary essay to explain his admiration for Sand: profound inwardness, austere sincerity, delicate feeling for nature, and melancholic eloquence of style. Moreover, Sénancour's appeal lay in the stir within him "of all the main forces by which modern life is and has been impelled": the "dissolving agencies" of the eighteenth century, the turmoil of French Revolution, and a vague promise of a better world to come. Arnold added that his own day was closer to bringing this new world about than was Sénancour's own time, an idea Arnold shared with Sand.

In "Stanzas in Memory of the Author of 'Obermann,' " Arnold turns from nature in the Alps—torrents familiar to readers of Sénancour's works—to the problem of human suffering, then to Sénancour, who has scanned so well "the hopeless tangle of our age," that he becomes a symbol that lives on, like the spirit of the scholar-gipsy, one "whom the world could not tame."[21]

In "Obermann Once More" Arnold turns again from nature, as he revisits Glion, in Switzerland, to recall Obermann. Like the scholar-gipsy, Obermann appears in a dream and addresses Arnold in optimistic words that are in the spirit of George Sand's *Lettres d'un Voyageur,* which Arnold had read three years before in the *Revue des Deux Mondes.* The words are more optimistic even than Sénancour's writings would allow, although there is basis for optimism in his works:[22]

> "Despair not thou as I despair'd,
> Nor be cold gloom thy prison!

Forward the gracious hours have fared,
And see! the sun is risen!

. . . .

"What still of strength is left, employ
That end to help attain:
One common wave of thought and joy
Lifting mankind again!"

As the vision ends, Arnold returns to nature and the dawn of a new day, with all the optimism a new dawn implies. "Obermann Once More," therefore, has Arnold's favorite theme (explored in the "Stanzas from the Grande Chartreuse" and in many other poems) of the "wandering between two worlds," but in this poem he makes a decision that the poet can do more than bemoan; "Obermann" has the call for joy that "Empedocles" lacked.[23] The striking contrast between Arnold's two poems on Obermann is the hope in the latter. The first is a lament for the "two desires" that "toss about the poet's feverish blood." In the latter, if he has no concrete solution, he has a resolution: not to give in to despair. A need for such optimism Arnold shared with Sand, as copyings from Sand in his *Note-Books* reveal.

Iris Sells traces influences of Sand in two other poems, but her illustrations are too general to be very convincing. There can be little doubt, however, that Sénancour and Sand were much involved in Arnold's working his way out of difficulty in the matter of his religious doubt and the need for optimism. Tinker and Lowry see unconscious biography in "Obermann Once More," that Arnold was at work on a compromise that led to a new view of Christianity, which he developed after monumental readings in the works of many authors. After 1866 Arnold turned with energy to the task of spreading a new statement of religion among his fellow Englishmen. His *Literature and Dogma* (1873) strove to relieve British minds disturbed by the higher criticism, pointing out that the Bible was not a scientific work but a literary one, which, if properly understood, deals with man's conduct—and a proper way to achieve that conduct—rather than creeds.[24] Both Sand and Sénancour were among the contributors to this view. Sand's optimism gave Arnold more inspiration in finding a way to escape the dilemma than did Sénancour, who finally became to Arnold chiefly the means for him to go to something else; by the time Arnold finished with Sénancour, the French writer had been changed and utilized to propagate an idea which Arnold wished to preach, just as Sand, sifted through Arnold's mind, became a much different kind of writer than she appeared to John Wilson Croker in the *Quarterly Review.*

One finds further evidence that Sénancour's religious views were important to Arnold in a review Arnold wrote of an 1863 edition of Sénancour's *Obermann.* Published in the *Academy* in October 1869, Arnold's essay again describes Sénancour as a man worthy of receiving praise from "Madame George Sand and Monsieur Sainte-Beuve" and Arnold himself praises Sénancour for his religious views: Sénancour, we are told, had criticized organized religion for its failures, for offering absurd dogmas when man needed something much more majestic; moreover, organized religion had "fabricated, patched, experimented, altered; renewed I know not what incoherent multitude of trivial ceremonies and dogmas, more fitted to scandalize the weak than to edify them. This dubious mixture you have joined to a morality sometimes false, often exceedingly noble, and almost austere; the one single point in which you have shown sagacity." The trouble, Arnold quoted Sénancour, was that the patchwork of religion will not last much longer than the time society has spent in constructing it. To all this Arnold replied: "There is a passage to be meditated by the new Oecumenical Council!"[25]

Then, too, Lionel Trilling sees Sénancour and Sand as writers who helped Arnold resolve his difficulties concerning religion. Trilling suggests that Arnold had reasons for admiring Sand other than those he listed in his anniversary essay, the chief one being Sand's ability to emerge from religious doubt and still remain optimistic. Both Sand and Arnold had lost faith in the God of the popular creeds, but as Sand herself described the new religion that emerged: "The loss is not loss of religious sense . . . it is quite the contrary, it is a restitution of allegiance to the true Divinity. It is a step made in the direction of this Divinity, it is an abjuration of the dogmas which did him dishonour." Arnold surely meant this when he compared Sand's sense of religion with Wordsworth's when the latter spoke of a "presence that disturbs me with the joy of elevated thoughts." Sand's ideal, which always animated her, also inspired Arnold in his youth and fortified him in old age.[26] Trilling concludes a chapter entitled "Obermann Once More" with a detailed discussion of Mrs. Humphry Ward's *Robert Elsmere,* a novel by Arnold's niece, in which religious doubt is the subject of fiction. Elsmere's earliest teacher had been a reader of Sénancour; another had studied the rationalists. Elsmere finally left the church to preach a new kind of Christ; he stripped the church of dogma and all the orthodox trimmings and substituted a belief in love and service of one's fellowman.

But another theme in Sand to which Arnold responded, says Trilling, is the exaltation of woman and the claim that she is able to experience passion to a degree that man is either unwilling or unable to do. To support his thesis Trilling lists Stendhal, Gobineau, Ibsen, Shaw, and D. H. Lawrence, who have used variations of this theme. Arnold understood, Trilling says, that women look "for more than devotion, that they seek in those they love a strength that need not be always moral." To this notion, which Sand sums up, Trilling ties in Arnold's love affair with Marguerite. Trilling also comments on Arnold's picking one of Sand's especial themes, love as the basis of social life. According to Trilling, Arnold understood that by "love" Sand meant "social equality." To convert Englishmen to this idea, Arnold devoted much energy; his speech on "Equality," for example, was an attempt to popularize this view.[27]

As mentioned above, Arnold's most important criticism of Sand was published in the *Fortnightly* in 1877, when the first anniversary of Sand's death was drawing near.[28] There Arnold gave his reactions to her works and stated the qualities of her life that pleased him. He did not write a critical survey; rather, he stated that he did not intend to "go regularly through her productions, to classify and value them one by one," nor did he want to go through her works, picking out selections to amuse an English public whom he felt was either ignorant of Sand or indifferent to her. Instead he said that he wrote the article for those to whom Sand has been a "friend and a power" and for his own satisfaction. "It is for myself." Arnold thus sets aside one of the fallacies, the "personal fallacy," which he had stated in the "Study of Poetry" may become a stumbling block in one's study of literature.

He began by quoting a phrase from Sand which he took to be the ground-motif that runs through all her works: "the sentiment of the ideal life, which is none other than man's normal life as we shall some day know it."

As in much of Arnold's criticism, he assumed the role of a professor determined to correct public taste. Sand, he said, was much more than a teller of charming stories and a creator of interesting characters. Beyond that there was more, the "spirit" of Sand, and to know this spirit one does not have to read all of her; rather he picked four books he would have his readers know as her most representative works.

First he included the *Lettres d'un Voyageur,* which had won praise from many people—Mazzini, George Eliot, Elizabeth Browning, Charlotte Brontë, and Jane Carlyle. He listed next *Mauprat,* in which Sand idealizes married love for one person throughout a lifetime. The third of his choices was *François le Champi,* still a classic for its nature scenes and for its style. For the fourth he chose *Valvèdre,* which may have been in his mind because he had just read an appreciative essay on it by Frederick W. H. Myers.[29] Interestingly enough Arnold's choices did not include *Lélia,* which Iris Sells thinks of all Sand's works influenced him the most, nor did he include *Indiana* or

Valentine, Sand's earliest and most controversial works. It may be that he ignored some of Sand's works for the same reason that he loftily ignored her sexual vagaries: either they had no particular relevance to the audience concerned, or he overlooked them because he wanted to, as in later life he denied the existence in his youth of a real Marguerite. Even if one wishes to quarrel with Arnold's choices it is difficult to do so, for he has said that he was not examining all of the works, and he was writing for himself, to prove points about a motif that he himself had selected.

From these four works he says one can detect "all the principal elements" of Sand's literary creations. He identifies these elements: "the cry of agony and revolt, the trust in nature and beauty, and the aspiration towards a purged and renewed human society." These three elements evolve into Sand's search for the "sentiment of the ideal life," a search that Sand makes without ceasing and with absolute sincerity.

The cry of revolt passed away, Arnold said, as it did for Goethe—as it had indeed passed away for the generation that was thrilled by *Lélia* and *Valentine;* the memories of this phase of Sand, however, will never pass away. He quoted from Sand to demonstrate what he thought typical of this period, choosing Lélia's words as she bemoans her fate in her cell on the mountain of the Camaldoli and Sylvia's cry over Jacques by his glacier in Tyrol. "Life is arid and terrible, repose is a dream, prudence is useless; mere reason alone serves simply to dry up the heart; there is but one virtue, the eternal sacrifice of oneself."

Arnold then made an oblique reference to the irregularities in Sand's private life, quoting from the *Lettres d'un Voyageur* a passage in which Sand says she was born to love (a trait she identifies as her misfortune). The same passage tells how she became judged an enemy of society because she said merely that there were many people made miserable by marriage. Arnold expressed regret that Sand could not feel "light and hope and power" within herself to lead others, especially the ones she loved, and he quoted Sand's half-repentance, when she refers to her children's attitude of regret for "these much trumpeted duels . . . with custom and belief."

Arnold strongly commended Sand for saying that if one's search for a better world is ineffectual, it is the world's loss and not the seeker's. To compensate for the ineffectuality of the search, Sand turned in her endeavor to escape the reign of stupidity to her second "element," the love of nature: "George Sand is one of the few French writers who keep us closely and truly intimate with rural nature. She gives us the wild-flowers by their actual names,—snowdrop, primrose, columbine, iris, scabious."

Arnold then referred to *Valentine* but did not quote from it, claiming that the language defies translation. He quoted from Sand's introduction to *La Mare au Diable* and he concluded with praise for her closeness of contact with the country; yet he claimed her interest in humanity always emerged to dominate the final picture and that the central human being in the picture was the French peasant. From him, Sand hoped for the third "element"—the movement toward a renewed human society. Arnold thought Sand forgave the peasant for supporting the Empire because it meant peace and security while other political parties seemed to promise only more strife. In spite of some political backwardness, the peasant had moved forward toward equality, with an increase in self-respect and well-being. Arnold thought Sand should be forgiven too if she speaks with too much enthusiasm for this new found equality, for she has seen that it has given the peasant tact, good manners, probity, and has made him human. To this comment Arnold could not refrain from adding: "Some little variation on our own eternal trio of Barbarians, Philistines, Populace, or on the eternal solo of Philistinism among our brethren of the United States and the Colonies, is surely permissible."

Arnold concluded by stating that the multiplicity of Sand's works—"always fresh, always attractive, but poured out too lavishly and rapidly"—may be a hindrance to her fame, but he predicted permanence for this great writer whom England knew "very little and very ill."

> The immense vibration of George Sand's voice upon the ear of Europe will not soon die away. Her passions and her errors have been abundantly talked of. She left them behind her, and men's memory of her will leave them behind also. There will remain of her to mankind the sense of benefit and stimulus from the passage upon earth of that large and frank nature, of that large and pure utterance—the *large utterance of the early gods.*

Another article by Arnold in which Sand figures prominently is "Copyright," published in the *Fortnightly Review* in 1880, where Arnold referred to a proposal by Sand and her publisher Levy to win a bigger reading public by printing cheap books. This position was Arnold's in support of the Royal Commission on Copyright, which recommended a new copyright law. Arnold believed a new law would result in cheaper good books and would do away with the present inequities under which "a new novel by George Eliot costs a guinea and a half while a new novel by George Sand costs three shillings."

Closely allied to the anniversary essay of 1877 is Arnold's contribution to the *Pall Mall Gazette* on 12 August 1885, written when a statue was unveiled in memory of Sand at La Châtre, a little town in Berry, not far from Nohant. This article reveals very clearly Arnold's preference for Sand's brand of romanticism over the realism of any other French writers of the hour, and in it Arnold equated Sand with Wordsworth and Goethe. He also predicted that the future would bear him out in his preference for Sand over Balzac, a preference Arnold shared with George Henry Lewes, Charlotte Brontë, George Eliot, and others.

> She could hardly escape a statue but the present is not her hour. . . . Now is the hour of the naturalists and realists, of the great work, as it is called, and solid art of Balzac, which Monsieur Daudet and other disciples are continuing; not of the work of humanitarians and idealists like George Sand and her master Rousseau. The work, whether of idealists or realists, must stand for what it is worth, and must pay the penalty of its defects.[30]

Arnold believed that Sand admirably stated the conditions under which Rousseau produced his works: that Rousseau had within him the love of goodness and an enthusiasm for beauty but that he knew nothing of them to start with. She stated also that the "absence of moral education had prolonged the childhood of his spirit beyond the ordinary term," that the reigning philosophy of the time was not moralistic and, in its hatred of unjust restraints, it left out duty altogether. Yet Rousseau, more logical and more serious than other writers of his day, gradually saw that liberty was not all and that philosophy must have "virtue, a religion, a social law." Sand, Arnold said, wrote under much the same conditions; moreover she had to make the same discovery for herself about liberty and philosophy. Also like Rousseau, Sand had faults of declamation, repetition, and extravagance; but Sand's works and Rousseau's were not defective, for they were written out of "a love of goodness and a desire for beauty" rather than by the approved method of Balzac: a disinterested curiosity. Arnold disagreed with Taine, who argued that the greatest works are produced by "disinterested curiosity" and that Shakespeare's works, like Balzac's, were so produced.

He is mistaken. The motive of Shakespeare, the master-thought at the bottom of Shakespeare's production, is the same as the master-thought at the bottom of the production of Homer and Sophocles, Dante and Moliere, Rousseau and George Sand. With all the differences of manner, power, and performance between these makers, the governing motive is the same. It is the motive enunciated in the burden of the famous chorus in the *Agamemnon* . . . "Let the good prevail."[31]

If Arnold's argument seems weak and untenable, at least he was consistent with his philosophy of what literature ought to do for the reader. As Arnold stated in his "Preface to First Edition of Poems" (1853):

For the Muses, as Hesiod says, were born that they might be "a forgetfulness of evils, and a truce from cares": and it is not enough that the Poet should add to the knowledge of men, it is required of him also that he should add to their happiness. "All Art," says Schiller, "is dedicated to Joy, and there is no higher and no more serious problem, than how to make men happy. The right Art is that alone, which creates the highest enjoyment."

A poetical work, therefore, is not yet justified when it has been shown to be an accurate, and therefore interesting representation; it has to be shown also that it is a representation from which men can derive enjoyment.[32]

And in "Obermann Once More":

And yet men have such need of joy!
But joy whose grounds are true;
And joy that should all hearts employ
As when the past was new.[33]

That Balzac's motive was curiosity instead of joy results in Balzac's being limited; he delineates not the life of man but the life of the Frenchman of his times, the "*homme sensuel moyen*." Furthermore this motive of curiosity becomes blended with cupidity and lubricity. Arnold strongly objected to this characteristic, and he judged that Rousseau with all his faults is "more truly alive than Balzac, his work is more than Balzac's a real part of French literature. . . . And a hundred years hence George Sand, the disciple of Rousseau, with much of Rousseau's faults, but yet with Rousseau's great motive inspiring her—George Sand, to whom the French literature of to-day is backward to do honour—George Sand will have established her superiority to Balzac as incontestably as Rousseau."[34]

In Sand's "strenuous and mixed work" from 1832 to

her death, Arnold singled out *Mauprat, La Petite Fadette, Jean de la Roche,* and *Valvèdre* as representative novels. Then using the same technique he used in his poems, "Memorial Verses" and "Heine," Arnold linked Sand with two other writers to whom Sand emerged superior: if Goethe's work is the "greatest and wisest influence," and Wordsworth's is the "purest and most poetic," then Sand's is the "most varied and attractive." We shall not err in judgment of Sand, he says, if we adopt the poet's faith and "feel she is greater than we know."[35]

Critics have varied in their reactions to Arnold's exaggerated praise for Sand. George Saintsbury is the most forgiving, recognizing that Sand's storm and stress period was similar to Arnold's own, that her works succored him, and "it would be as just to blame him for thinking his mother more beautiful, his father wiser than they actually were." Herbert Paul blames the influence of Sainte-Beuve more than the influence of Sand to explain Arnold's lapses in taste, lapses that caused him to praise too highly people like the Guérins, almost on a par with Heine, Spinoza, and Marcus Aurelius. Yet Paul praises Arnold's essay on Sand as "a charming memorial tribute" and thinks it is a shame that Sand is not much read in England, although he doubts if Sand ever brought the *vie idéale* that Arnold so admired down to earth, down to the real.[36]

E. K. Brown tends to deprecate Arnold's estimate of Sand, noting even if Arnold called her and Heine the chief figures in European literature in the quarter century after 1830, that Arnold was always emphatic that this was an unrewarding century both in thought and art.[37] It is true, of course, that Arnold did not fully appreciate Wordsworth's "Intimation Ode," or Keats's "Pot of Basil," and that Tennyson may have been the model for these lines in "Scholar-Gipsy":

> and amongst us one,
> Who most has suffer'd, takes dejectedly
> His seat upon the intellectual throne;
> And all his store of sad experience he
> Lays bare of wretched days;
> Tells us his misery's birth and growth and signs,
> And how the dying spark of hope was fed,
> And how the breast was soothed, and how the head,
> And all his hourly varied anodynes.
>
> This for our wisest!

Brown thinks that Arnold's audience or the casual reader would not be likely to recall that Arnold had so poor an opinion of the writings of his contemporaries that his praise of Sand and of Heine is of "almost pitifully small account."[38] Although Brown's comments may help give some proportion to Arnold's critical estimate of Sand, they greatly underestimate his admiration for her. Arnold may have decried the mediocre production of contemporaries, but when he evaluated Sand's contribution to himself and to his age, he could rarely refrain from hyperbole. His letters and the anniversary essay seem to support this conclusion, as do the copyings in his *Note-Books*.[39]

There are numerous passages copied from Sand's works in Arnold's *Note-Books;* they are surpassed in number only by passages from Goethe, *De Imitatione Christi*, Sainte-Beuve, Bishop Thomas Wilson, and the Bible. Arnold referred to twelve of Sand's works; and it is known that he owned copies of at least five of them. Typical of Arnold's practice, he returned many times to a favorite passage, to recopy one he had previously written down. Thus the line "The healthful habits of maturity," from Sand's *La Daniella,* appears first in 1859, again in 1862, 1864 (henceforth he punctuated the line with an exclamation mark), 1865, 1866, and 1867. The same quotation is also found twice in *Note-Book No. 1.*

Arnold began copying passages into the *Note-Books* in 1852. The first passage from Sand occurs in 1856; of five passages copied that year, one is from Sand, her *Histoire de ma Vie,* in which she discusses the true nature of prayer.[40] After 1859 Arnold drew more heavily on Sand: quotations abound from *La Daniella* (six in all) dealing primarily with poetry as an emotional release and all expressing a desire for achieving stability in life. In addition to the line about the "healthful habits of maturity," one long quotation deals with artists who were inspired and who produced even though they were in spiritual torment. Arnold adopted one passage from Sand to fit his own needs: Sand had written that she danced "to free my spirit and my feet from the ground I walk on." The quotation substitutes "Je fais des vers" (I write poetry) for the verb *dance.*[41] A long passage from *L'Homme de Neige,* in 1860, advises against being discouraged and disturbed about the future. In this passage Sand speaks of forsaking worldly ambitions and of scorning mistakes (made when one is young and sometimes frivolous), and she advises seeking salvation in a Carlylean manner: work, some twelve hours a day of it, "possible to anyone who is not wretched and unwell."[42]

By 1871 Sand's spell over Arnold had lessened. Of 190 passages in the *Note-Book* that year, only one is from Sand, a passage that advises one to think of nothing in life that is not connected with the "amelioration of morals and the reconciliation of interests."[43] Nor are there re-copyings that year of favorite passages.

Passages in 1873 and in 1876 relate to one of Arnold's favorite themes: calmness arrived at out of morality, after the writer has conquered despair. One passage advises that "one must rearrange in order to take the lofty view." In 1877 there occurs the passage from Sand's *Journal d'un Voyageur,* "The need to love, the sentiment of the ideal life which is none other than the normal life such as we are called to know it."[44] This line Arnold took for the motif of his anniversary essay on Sand published in the same year.

In 1882, as Arnold drew to the close of his life, he became newly interested in Sand through her mystical novel *Spiridion.* Passages that year are many—thirty-four from Sand, all from *Spiridion.* Typical is a passage that comments how much more difficult it is to build up (*batir*) than it is to tear down (*abattre*) or the passage that sums up theology: "belief, hope, love."[45] One significant passage on old age contrasts optimistically with Arnold's poem "Growing Old." In his own poem, first published in 1867, the last years of life are characterized:

> Deep in our hidden heart
> Festers the dull remembrance of a change,
> But no emotion—none.

Yet the passage from Sand's *Spiridion,* which struck Arnold, states: "Instead of growing morally colder with old age, I feel my heart, vivified and renewed, rejuvenated to the degree that my body leans toward destruction." One wonders if Arnold had changed his mind or whether the conflicting views are a part of his complexity.

Arnold continued copying passages in the *Note-Books* almost until his death. The last passage from Sand is in 1884 from *Jacques* and it adds an optimistic note: Florence asks Jacques if the world is still far from the "shining summit." Jacques replies that the answer is God's secret, but their world is much closer to perfection than that of "all the people who preceded us."[46] One last quotation from Sand, undated, in *General Note-Book No. 1* Arnold combines into a single long passage with quotations from the works of two other writers: *The Manava Dharma Sastra* or *Institutes of Menu,* translated by Sir William Jones, and Rousseau's *Julie* or *Nouvelle Héloïse.* Significantly, the whole passage concerns Sand's successful quest for a satisfactory substitute to replace outworn creeds. The quotation from Jones's translation of the *Institutes of Menu* refers to people who have a "lively feeling for the worthless morals of our time and who have a desire to remedy them;" the quotation from *Julie* calls for a "return to the depths of our conscience" to find a principle on which we can establish an immovable "basis of our conduct"; the passage from Sand's *Histoire de ma Vie* speaks of "a delightful absolute confidence" which inundates one once he denies earthly pleasures and aspires to heavenly ones.[47]

The very last passage from Sand in *Note-Book No. 2* is from the *Correspondance,* a letter of Sand's written in August 1837, and it is a cry from the heart that Arnold in his anniversary essay called the first "element" of Sand's works: "Mon Dieu, mon dieu, how I wept, how I stifled my complaints, how I concealed my trouble."[48]

Interestingly enough, of these eleven books from which Arnold copied most frequently, only one is among the four he recommended to the readers of his anniversary essay as Sand's most representative works. That is *Mauprat*. Likewise *Mauprat* is the only one of Sand's works mentioned in the 1884 essay from which passages appear in the *Note-Books*.

In addition to these passages copied from Sand, the *Note-Books* contain additional evidence that the French writer was often on Arnold's mind. In the *Note-Books* Arnold listed volumes he meant to read. Some are crossed off as read; often a book title will be repeated from year to year, indicating that the world was often too much with Arnold for him to fulfill his best intentions.

In 1876 Arnold reminded himself in the *Note-Books* to write an article on Sand. His ideas developed into the anniversary essay. In 1877 Sand was still on his mind as an author to continue reading: he lists *Lettres pendant la guerre* and *Mauprat* again. That year he noted as completed his writing on Sand.

In 1880 he listed *Dernières Lettres* among books to take to Fox How, and later that year he listed the book as read, along with *François le Champi*—which must have been a rereading, for he had praised the beginning of that book in a letter to Clough in 1848. Arnold listed also *La Petite Fadette* to be read in that year of 1880. The next year he cited three books by Sand to be read, *Questions d'art et de Littérature, Légendes Rustiques,* and *Le Diable aux*

Champs. That year he listed Sand as an author to be read "for the holidays"; at the same time he reminded himself to read Hartman, Eckermann, Goethe, the *Odyssey*, Bossuet, the Prayer Book, and Burke.

In 1882 he listed "G.S. and Epict on happiness" and *Spiridion* as read, and the *Questions d'art* as still to be read. In 1883 among books listed "for America" he included *Diable aux Champs*, which he later, in 1884, noted as read. Concerned with reading or rereading Sand up to his death, he recorded as read in 1886 volumes one and two of the *Correspondance* and *Contes d'une Grand-Mère*. In 1888, his last year, Arnold listed volumes five and six of the *Correspondance* and Caro's biography of Sand to be read. One of the last entries, in February 1888, was to read "G. Sand, V ——." The volume number is missing. That same month, along with Sand, he listed Milton and Shakespeare's sonnets.

Thus the *Note-Books* furnish evidence of Sand's importance to Arnold, as his letters, poetry, and essays attest to his participation in the cult of George Sand. Yet the passages in the *Note-Books* reveal even better than do any of his other writings what Sand meant to him. In Arnold's mind George Sand was changed into a person much like Arnold himself: the melancholic artist, dissatisfied with the age, yet determined, at the cost of great spiritual exertion, to throw off despair and correct the evils of the world.

IX

Appreciations in Retrospect

> Not being Romantics, we can no longer experience the same thrill.
> Curtis Cate

> A shrewd one it will be who will unravel my mother.
> Sand's daughter, Solange

Matthew Arnold's major essay on George Sand is "an appreciation," a critical genre with which some twentieth-century readers may not be in sympathy. Arnold acted as a critic whom nature had endowed with uncommon sensitivity. He reflected on Sand's works and responded without an explication of any single text and without a search for relationships within the text, expounding only on its aesthetic and ethical influence on the reader as his *magister vitae,* his director of life. This charming and somewhat naive point of view is typically Victorian.

That Englishmen in the Victorian Age looked upon literary figures as sages is readily documented.[1] Literary works replaced the Bible as a guide to give solutions to problems, personal and cosmic. Wilkie Collins satirizes the tradition in *The Moonstone:* in times of crisis the servant Betteredge turns to Defoe's *Robinson Crusoe,* quoting passages that he feels prophesy and illuminate present situations. Betteredge praises the method and the book: "I have found it my friend in need in all the necessities of this mortal life. When my spirits are bad—Robinson Crusoe. When I want advice—Robinson Crusoe. In past times, when my wife plagued me; in present times, when I have had a drop too much—Robinson Crusoe. I have worn out six stout Robinson Crusoes with hard work in my service."[2]

Arnold, who did more than any other writer in the nineteenth century to dignify criticism,[3] took literary works as seriously as did thousands of other English, European, and American readers of Sand. Writing of another romantic writer—Byron—Arnold commented: "With shivering heart the strife we saw / Of passion with eternal law" and moralized: "He taught us little; but our soul / Had *felt* him like the thunder's roll."[4] Arnold and his fellow Englishmen were similarly fascinated by Sand's titanic struggle with convention. But Sand taught much. Interest in her and in her works was at such a peak from 1830 to 1860 that the period could be called the "Age of Sand" as one speaks of the "Age of Byron." But with Sand a new ingredient was added—her femininity. When Elizabeth Browning called her the greatest female genius of any country or age, she did not mean that there were greater male geniuses but that Sand was the greatest and a woman. Sand's reputation was enhanced beyond all proportion by her admirers because of her sex. At the same time, her enemies applied to her a double standard; when she failed to live up to the exalted standards conservatives had designated to her sex, she was all the more condemned.

No doubt Sand's attack on the institution of marriage as she understood it and had endured it under the Napoleonic code brought about most of her notoriety in Victorian England. Rightly F. W. Myers observes that the championing of free love in her own life and through the characters in her novels often made her "a word of fear" in British households.[5]

Like modern readers, the Victorians were fascinated by Sand's numerous liaisons. One critic, attempting to estimate the number of Sand's affairs, gave up, crying out, "Spare me the census."[6] But unlike modern audiences, the Victorians were not much interested in the specter of homosexuality in Sand's private life, and there is no homosexuality in the lives of the characters in her novels. In this instance the Victorians were probably closer to the truth about Sand's sexual life than the twentieth-century commentators who have morbidly exaggerated a latent lesbian tendency in Sand. An example of such distortion is found in the recent British television series suggestively entitled "That Notorious Woman," in which Rosemary Harris, as Sand, appeared lovelier than Sand probably ever did. And in his new biography Joseph Barry pictures Sand musing on Byron's "open secret," which Barry interprets as Byron's bisexuality, and Barry chides Sandists for their tendency "to reduce the heat of that contact [between Sand and actress Marie Dorval] to a warm friendship."[7] Or again take Mario Praz's statement in *The Romantic Agony* that lesbianism increased in England after the advent of George Sand.[8] Actually Praz's is one of those statements, not uncommon to scholars, that read well until they are closely examined. Praz may have gathered evidence from various Victorian sources—like the comment Jane Carlyle made after her friend Geraldine Jewsbury had flirted in Jane's presence: "I wondered she should expect me to behave decently to her after she had for a whole evening been making love before my very face to *another man*,"[9]—but there is no evidence that George Sand was the sole inspiration. Moreover, Sand's best French biographer, André Maurois, refers to lesbianism only obliquely, and Sand's recent American biographer, Curtis Cate, doubts that Sand was inveterately lesbian.[10] In their press the Victorians sometimes saw Sand as nymphomanic but not homosexual, in part perhaps because of their reluctance to discuss the matter in public. The press chiefly refers to Sand's "hermaphrodite dress" or to her masculine talent for smoking cigars.

Sand's image as a notorious woman intrigued her Victorian enemies and compelled them to write denunciations, sometimes outrageous, in defense of Victorian womanhood. Yet the most impressive shadow Sand cast was among those very women who saw her as a living symbol of their own longing for emancipation. Often, as in the lives of Elizabeth Barrett and George Eliot, Sand was the source of strength for bold action.

Indeed Aurore Dupin Dudevant, alias George Sand, was an important part of French life when France was fulfilling the role it has played for centuries, the battleground for conflicting political and social philosophies. In many ways Sand was the vanguard in the fight to create the proper setting for the emergence of the modern woman. She appeared on the literary scene when women's rights needed to be questioned, and she played an important role in that questioning. Sand was a major force in the nineteenth century, and she had the good fortune to appear as a novelist when the novel became the leading literary genre for a rapidly expanding middle class; her second stroke of luck was to appear in Paris when that city offered leadership to the elite of the literary world.

The feminist side of Sand merges with another that guaranteed her fame in Victorian England, in Europe, and in the United States: her image as a militant and idealistic social reformer championing the rights of the working class. It is no surprise that the American Julia Ward Howe, who espoused world peace, female emancipation, and the abolition of slavery, and who stirred her fellow citizens with the "Battle Hymn of the Republic" was herself stirred by Sand. Her favorite review, pirated by a British publication, is a good example of political bias spilling over into literary judgment. Howe represents a liberal, favorable review of Sand, just as John Wilson Croker represents a conservative, unfavorable reaction. The tendency to let political bias influence literary evaluations is further exemplified by Bertha Thomas, who was Sand's first English biographer. Mrs. Thomas not only attempted to make Sand's politics palatable to England, but she explained away all of Sand's eccentricities. Thus Mrs. Thomas writes that masculine dress was a necessity dictated by the muddy country roads of Berry, where male attire was practical, or by the night life of Paris, where masculine dress brought safety and a greater degree of freedom to attend lectures. Mrs. Thomas minimizes Sand's smoking, mentioning only that no imitator of Sand gained by adopting the habit. Some of Sand's lovers, for example Dr. Pagello and Michel de Bourges, are not mentioned. In Sand's relationships with Musset and with Chopin, she emerges under Mrs. Thomas's pen more as a worthy nurse than anything else. Explaining Sand's career as an emancipated woman writer, she quotes Sand as saying that she used the "scribe's pen" rather than the "housekeeper's needle" to support her children. Her cover-up of all Sand's eccentricities is an excellent example of an attempt to transform Sand into a "right minded artist" (to use Ruskin's term). That right-mindedness was necessary if most Victorians could view Sand as an artist who could lead them to a better life.

John Stuart Mill regarded Sand as a serious political observer, and rightly so. Consider Sand's observation in the revolutionary *Bulletin de la République:* "If the majority possesses the truth of the present, the minority holds the truth of the future."[11] That sentiment was compatible with the thinking of Emerson and Mill. In his most famous essay, "Self-Reliance," in 1841, Emerson had written: "Society everywhere is in conspiracy against the manhood of everyone of its members." And Mill, in his *On Liberty,* wrote in 1859: "If all mankind minus one, were of one opinion, and only one person were of the contrary opinion, mankind would be no more justified in silencing that one person, than he, if he had the power, would be justified in silencing mankind." In 1886 Ibsen was expounding on the same theme Sand had expressed in 1848.[12] Yet no critic claims that Sand was a great politician offering intellectual leadership. Indeed Mazzini stated that Sand had no firm political faith; instead he claimed that her writings were only the "passive echo of an artist, the echo of a faith not truly hers."[13] Still, Sand's association with politicians of the left and her zeal for reform enlarged her image and her impact on the Victorians.

When one tries to analyze why the Victorians were fascinated by Sand, the evidence of her appeal as a symbol of the emancipated woman or her appeal as a political symbol is likely to overwhelm. But the Victorians very much appreciated Sand the writer, the literary artist who could create characters, describe nature, and entertain. This is no doubt how Sand saw herself. Prosper Merimée gossiped of Sand's leaving his bed, the only night they spent together, to begin work on her next novel before the dying coals in the fireplace. Sand felt compelled to write, and her more than one hundred volumes represent her real fulfillment. Victorians who well understood the value of literature to entertain and to instruct took no contemporary foreign writer more seriously.

It is now more than a hundred years since Sand's death. Was her fame merely faddish and passing or was it well established and deserved? Actually anyone who has weighed the evidence objectively will reply that Sand's fame was deserved. Her novels satisfied so great a proportion of discerning Victorians that readers in the twentieth century may not easily dismiss Sand. Those skeptical of her literary worth may begin with the pastoral novels, *La Mare au Diable, La Petite Fadette,* and *François le Champi,* although these novels lose much of their charm when translated. From these novels most readers will agree that the elaborate praise of Sand's style by George Eliot, Matthew Arnold, and Henry James, among others, was deserved. With their scrupulous attention to the particularities of the French countryside, these pastoral novels may even please devotees of writers of local color. A modern reader with Victorian fortitude might then tackle

Countess of Rudolstadt; as a Gothic tale it still holds up, in spite of a hazy mysticism uncharacteristic of Sand. After these, to understand Sand as a part of French romanticism, he should read *Lélia* in the original or in translation,[14] and if still interested, he can find in the extensive canon of George Sand an opportunity to make his own evaluation to test Victorian response to her work.

Sand remains an international figure. Tourists still visit Sand's chateau in Nohant, much as Matthew Arnold did in 1842. Though Nohant is more accessible now than it was in Arnold's day, the chateau still seems remote. At nearby Chenonceau an avenue is named after her; a café there bears her name; a local newspaper at Chenonceau prints serially a cartoon version of her novels. Beyond Nohant, at La Châtre, stands the statue dedicated to the good lady of Nohant.

The chateau itself is a national shrine. A guide points out memorabilia, from huge pots in the kitchen where the domestic Sand prepared preserves, to the attic where mementos of the militant and romantic Sand are preserved: her writing desk and a cast of her arm. On the ground floor the dining table is set with place cards for Turgenev, Alexandre Dumas, and other greats who dined there. In the same room there is a piano on which Liszt played. Outside the wall lies the bare graveyard where Sand is buried, and in a kind of square there is a dilapidated church that seems to symbolize an age that had declined even in Sand's time. Readers who share some of the idealism Sand tried to generate may want to ask whether the answers given by succeeding thinkers have been any more satisfactory for the happiness and well being of the human race. Whatever their answer, George Sand will continue to be the subject of biographies and studies: a remarkable woman in a century noted for uncommon people.

Notes

CHAPTER I

1. Marcel Moraud, *Le Romantisme Français en Angleterre de 1814 à 1848,* p. 205.

2. André Maurois, *Lélia, The Life of George Sand,* p. 15.

3. Frances Winwar, *Life of the Heart,* pp. 214, 265.

4. Oscar Wilde, *The Picture of Dorian Gray,* p. 12.

5. For a study of Sand's influence on Whitman, see Esther Shephard, *Walt Whitman's Pose.*

6. Mazzini, *Life and Writings,* 6: 56.

7. Gordon Haight, ed., *The George Eliot Letters,* 1: 277.

8. [J. W. Croker], "French Novels," *Quarterly Review* 56: 66.

9. Mary Margaret Blair Busk was a frequent contributor to *Blackwood's, Athenaeum,* and *Foreign Quarterly Review.* Her brother was a professor of English language and literature at University College, London, from 1831 to 1834, and she frequently lived on the Continent with her husband, William Busk, who was a barrister and at one time a member of Parliament.

10. He believed in being tolerant of the vagaries of "Genius." His preface to *Conti, The Discarded* made a plea for "Genius" to be taken on its own terms and not to be bound by the rules for ordinary people.

11. Clarence Decker, *The Victorian Conscience,* p. 9. Decker's work deals with the critical reception in Victorian England of Balzac, Baudelaire, Zola, Daudet, Ibsen, and the Russian novelists. He makes slight mention of Sand.

12. Mazzini, "George Sand," *The People's Journal* 3: 131–34.

13. Moraud, p. 49.

14. *Sharpe's London Magazine* (incorporated with *The Illustrated Magazine)* 27: 15; *Atlantic Monthly* 8: 513–34.

15. Betty Miller, ed. *Elizabeth Barrett to Miss Mitford,* p. 147; letter dated 27 November 1842.

16. Walter E. Houghton, *The Victorian Frame of Mind, 1830–1870,* p. 364.

CHAPTER II

1. *National Review* 6: 38.

2. "French Novels," *Quarterly Review* 56: 99.

3. Patrick Kennedy, "The Life, Eccentricities, and Literature of George Sand," *Dublin University Magazine* 61: 220, 232–33. Kennedy (1801–1873) owned a bookshop in London and taught in Dublin.

4. *Bentley's Quarterly Review* 2: 382.

5. *People's Journal* 3: 134.

6. *Foreign Quarterly Review* 14: 145 (Am. ed.).

7. *Paris and the Parisians,* 2: 259–60. (Mrs. Trollope was despised in America for her caustic comments in *Domestic Manners of the Americans,* published in 1832.)

8. "Madame Sand and the New Apocalypse," *Paris Sketch Book of Mr. M. A. Titmarsh,* p. 193. Thackeray's notes were first published in 1840.

9. Quoted from Houghton, *Victorian Frame of Mind,* p. 420; original article appeared in *Literary and Social Judgements* 1: 188, 225.

10. Richard K. P. Pankhurst, *The Saint-Simonians, Mill and Carlyle,* pp. 2–5, 23, et passim. (*OED* defines *scortatory* as pertaining to or consisting of fornication or lewdness.)

11. Pankhurst, p. 47. Quoted from *Alfred, Lord Tennyson, a memoir by his son,* 1: 98–99.

12. *Quarterly Review* 56: 69, 102.

13. Ibid., p. 129.

14. *Paris and the Parisians in 1835,* 2: 259ff.; Frances Eleanor Trollope, *A Memoir of Frances Trollope,* 1: 243, et passim.

15. *Paris Sketch Book,* p. 193.

16. *Athenaeum,* no. 723: 687–89.

17. "The Abbé de la Mennais," *Foreign Quarterly Review* 21: 71 (Am. ed.).

18. "Rousseau's *Nouvelle Héloïse* and the Modern Literature Extravagant," *Foreign Quarterly Review* 27: 71 (Am. ed.).

19. "Parisian Morals and Manners," *Edinburgh Review* 77: 60 (Am. ed.); *Blackwood's* 64: 568.

20. "Oeuvres Completes de George Sand," *Foreign and Colonial Quarterly Review* 10: 480–81.

21. "On Romanticism and on the Present State of French Literature," *Wesleyan Methodist Magazine* 70: 267, 356.

22. *North British Review* 98: 159.

23. See April 1836 *Quarterly Review* article on French novels; *London and Westminster Review* 3 and 25 (July 1836): 167–73 (Am. ed.); this was the first volume of the combined *London Review* and *Westminster Review.*

24. "George Sand," *People's Journal* 3: 132–34.

25. In a January 1869 letter to George William Curtis. Haight, *Letters,* 5: 8.

26. [George Henry Lewes], "Complete Works of George Sand," *Foreign Quarterly Review* 32: 145–63 (Am. ed.).

27. Ibid., 145ff.

28. Haight, *Letters,* 2: 258.

29. *Foreign Quarterly Review* 37: 19 (Am. ed.).

30. *National Review* 6: 52–55.

31. "George Sand," *Saturday Review* 14: 194.

32. "French Novelists," *London Society* 21: 146ff.

33. *Blackwood's Edinburgh Magazine* 121: 83–84. Shand (1832–1907) was a journalist and critic who also practiced law. See Haight, *Letters,* 5: 362.

34. Frederic W. Maitland, *The Life and Letters of Leslie Stephen,* pp. 307–8.

35. *The Works of John Ruskin,* 29: 588, 34: 376.

36. "George Sand," *Nineteenth Century* 1: 299.

CHAPTER III

1. Miller, pp. 226–28; letter dated 1844.

2. Frederick G. Kenyon, ed., *Letters of Elizabeth Barrett Browning,* 1: 233, 303. For further evidence of Sand's influence on Mrs. Browning, see chap. 6 below.

3. Haight, *Letters,* 1: 277–78.

4. *Le Romantisme Français en Angleterre,* p. 400.

5. Emilie and Georges Romieu, *The Life of George Eliot,* p. 63.

6. Haight, *Letters,* 2: 91.

7. *Calvacade of the English Novel,* p. 316.

8. E. C. Gaskell, *The Life of Charlotte Brontë,* pp. 318–19.

9. J. L. Halliday, *Mr. Carlyle My Patient,* p. 58. This interesting if dubious attempt to psychoanalyze Carlyle from his works has interpreted Jane Welsh as Carlyle may have seen her —masculine in education, masculine in some of her physical traits, and masculine in her literary and intellectual interests.

10. *Literary Recollections,* pp. 205–6.

11. Leonard Huxley, *Jane Welsh Carlyle,* p. 132; Trudy Bliss, *Jane Welsh Carlyle,* p. 100.

12. Lawrence and Elizabeth Hanson, *Necessary Evil,* p. 417.

13. Ibid., pp. 269–70.

14. Harry Rudman, *Italian Nationalism and English Letters,* p. 444.

15. Hanson, *Necessary Evil,* p. 260.

16. Huxley, *Jane Welsh Carlyle,* p. 38.

17. Townsend Scudder, *Jane Welsh Carlyle,* pp. 351–52. When *Adam Bede* was first published John Blackwood, the publisher, suspected that Jane Carlyle was the author, for Lewes had arranged to have copies sent to Froude, Dickens, Thackeray, Ruskin, and Jane Carlyle. Since Jane was the only woman in the group, Blackwood suspected this was a ruse to cover up her identity.

18. Bliss, *Jane Welsh Carlyle,* pp. 249–50.

19. Susanne Howe, *Geraldine Jewsbury,* p. 80.

20. Ibid., pp. 47–48.
21. Ibid., pp. 105, 23, 43.
22. *Foreign Quarterly Review* 27: 71.
23. Elizabeth Schermerhorn, *Seven Strings of the Lyre*, p. 216.
24. *Victorian Frame of Mind,* p. 359.
25. See Francis Mineka, *Dissidence of Dissent,* pp. 290–91.
26. Dickens wrote about Collins in 1853: "He occasionally expounds a code of morals, taken from French novels, which I instantly and with becoming gravity smash." Robert Ashley, *Wilkie Collins* (New York: Roy Publishers, 1952), p. 39.
27. Diane Johnson, *Lesser Lives,* p. 47.

CHAPTER IV

1. Maurois, *Lélia,* p. 206.
2. Liszt at this time (1835) persuaded the Countess d'Agoult, who was carrying his child, to leave her husband and become his common-law wife. They visited Sand at Nohant. Although Sand and the Countess fell out from time to time, the three kept up a long friendship. The Countess herself turned author under the pen name Daniel Stern.
3. At about this same time in America, Edgar Allan Poe used the concept of metempsychosis in "Morella," "Ligeia," and "A Tale of the Ragged Mountains." As a critic Poe was much interested in a book by R. M. Bird, *Sheppard Lee,* in which the chief character inhabits seven different bodies of persons who had died. See Robert Jacobs, *Poe, Journalist and Critic* (Baton Rouge: Louisiana State University Press, 1969), p. 173.
4. Winwar, pp. 273–74.
5. Where one former lover, Prosper Merimée, voted for her and another former lover, Jules Sandeau, voted against Sainte-Beuve's proposal to honor Sand with an award of twenty thousand francs. Maurois, pp. 394–95. Francis Gribble disputes this fact in his biography, *George Sand and Her Lovers,* saying Sandeau was not present at the time the vote was taken.
6. *Blackwood's* was not favorable to Talleyrand but may

have printed the article because of its thesis, that all politics is vanity; furthermore *Blackwood's* liked Talleyrand's compliment to the Duke of Wellington and his scorn of Palmerston.

7. *Quarterly Review* 56: 66–67.

8. Ibid., pp. 100–101.

9. Perhaps the day of publication (Saint George's Day) was the reason for the anglicized first name; the last was shortened from Sandeau. Karenine in her biography thinks "Georges" appealed to Sand as a synonym of "Berrichon," a name given to a group of young people from Berry province with whom Sand associated in Paris during the 1830s. She continued to write "Georges" until 1833; after that her first name became "George." Karenine, 1: 341. In *Histoire de ma Vie* Sand speaks of the selection of her pen name and gives "Georges" as the first writing. Curtis Cate in his biography, *George Sand* (p. 203), attributes the selection of "Georges" to Sand's thought that the name, being descended from *georgos* (husbandman), would be a suitable pseudonym for a writer who came from the Berry province and who was close to the land.

10. See John A. R. Marriott, *The Makers of Modern Italy*, pp. 1–25.

11. Schermerhorn, p. 212.

12. Where one evening Mazzini read to his fellow exiles Browning's "An Italian in England," to show how a British liberal could sympathize with the Young Italy movement.

13. *Monthly Chronicle* 4: 25.

14. *Life and Letters*, 6: 46.

15. Joseph Rossi, *The Image of America in Mazzini's Writings*, p. 52.

16. Schermerhorn, p. 214.

17. "George Sand's Recent Reviews," *Foreign Quarterly Review* 37: 17 (Am. ed.).

18. *Eclectic Review* 7: 539.

19. *Athenaeum* no. 723: 688.

20. *Foreign Quarterly Review* 31: 102.

21. *Foreign and Colonial Quarterly Review* 1: 492–94.

22. "The Macaulay Election of 1846, containing comments

on the Macaulay Rejection of 1847," *Quarterly Review* 81: 533. The "editrix" referred to was probably Matilda Hays.

23. *National Review* 6: 39–64.

24. Haight, *Letters,* 1: 254.

25. Ibid., 2: 5.

26. Kenyon, 1: 426.

27. Howard Foster Lowry, ed., *The Letters of Matthew Arnold to Arthur Clough,* p. 20.

28. Ibid., pp. 58–59.

29. Ibid., p. 59.

30. Ibid., p. 79.

31. Trilling, *Matthew Arnold,* p. 347.

32. Howard Foster Lowry, Karl Young, and Waldo Hillary Dunn, eds., *The Note-Books of Matthew Arnold,* p. 10.

33. Maurois, p. 451.

34. Maitland, *The Life and Letters of Leslie Stephen,* pp. 307–8.

CHAPTER V

1. "The New Classic Drama in France," *Foreign Quarterly Review* 36: 19 (Am. ed.).

2. *London Society* 21: 146.

3. Miller, *Elizabeth Barrett to Miss Mitford,* p. 157.

4. Ruskin, *Works,* 34: 378; Morley, *Critical Miscellanies,* 3: 49; James, "George Sand," *Galaxy* 24: 51 (This American magazine praised Bertha Thomas's biography of Sand when it was published in Boston in 1891 by reprinting a very appreciative article on Sand that it had published in 1870); Maurois, *Lélia,* p. 401. Naturally not all writers were fascinated by Sand's language. Compare the views of Nietzsche, who characterized Sand as "*lactea ubertas*—in translation, the milk cow with 'a beautiful style.'" (The quotation marks around "beautiful style" are Nietzsche's.) He says elsewhere about Sand: "I read the first Lettres d'un Voyageur. Like everything that is descended from Rousseau, false, fabricated, bellows, exaggerated. I cannot stand this motley wallpaper style any more than the

mob aspiration for generous feelings. The worst feature, to be sure, is the female's coquetry with male attributes, with the manners of naughty boys. How cold she must have been throughout, this insufferable artist! She wound herself like a clock and wrote. Cold, like Hugo, like Balzac, like all the romantics as soon as they took up poetic invention. And how self-satisfied she may have lain there all the while, this fertile writing-cow who had in her something German in the bad sense, like Rousseau himself, her master, and who in any case was possible only during the decline of French taste! But Renan reveres her." Quoted from "Skirmishes of an Untimely Man," in *Twilight of the Idols,* pp. 513, 516.

5. Horatio F. Brown, *John Addington Symonds,* p. 210.

6. *British and Foreign Review* 8: 368.

7. "The Works of George Sand," *Foreign Quarterly Review* 32: 145–63, and "George Sand's Recent Novels," *Foreign Quarterly Review* 37: 12–20. Quotations in the following paragraphs are from vol. 32.

8. *Works,* 24: 378.

9. Decker, *Victorian Conscience,* p. 150. In Norse mythology the *Ragnorôk* is the final destruction of the world.

10. Maurois, p. 419.

11. Ibid., p. 46.

12. *People's Journal* 3: 136.

13. *Life and Writings,* 6: 56–57.

14. J. W. Cross, *Life of George Eliot,* p. 86.

15. *National Review* 6: 57.

16. Winwar, p. 213.

17. Maurois, p. 454.

CHAPTER VI

1. Miller, pp. 144–45; letter dated November 1842.

2. Ibid., p. 158; letter dated 28 December 1842.

3. The volume was published in America in October of that year under the title *A Drama of Exile: And Other Poems.* Her other volumes, previously published, were *Essay on Mind; with*

other Poems (1826) and *The Seraphim and Other Poems* (1838). In addition she had published a translation of Aeschylus's *Prometheus Bound* (1838).

4. Miller, pp. 225–26; letter dated September 1844.

5. Ibid., p. 240.

6. Gardner B. Taplin, *The Life of Elizabeth Barrett Browning*, p. 139.

7. Ernest de Selincourt, *The Letters of William and Dorothy Wordsworth*, 3: 1293–94; letter addressed to Edward Moxon.

8. Kenyon, 1: 303.

9. Alexander Carlyle, ed., *Letters of Thomas Carlyle to John Stuart Mill, John Sterling and Robert Browning*, pp. 286–87.

10. Thurman L. Hood, ed., *Letters of Robert Browning*, p. 36.

11. Kenyon, 2: 26; letter dated 22 October 1851 from Paris.

12. Ibid., p. 29.

13. Ibid., pp. 55–57.

14. Ibid., pp. 59–60.

15. Paul Landes and Ronald Freeman, eds., *Letters of the Brownings to George Barrett*, p. 174; letter dated 28 February 1852.

16. Leonard Huxley, ed., *Elizabeth Barrett Browning: Letters to her Sister*, pp. 155–56; letter dated 3 March 1852.

17. Kenyon, 2: 62–64.

18. Dorothy Hewlett, *Elizabeth Barrett Browning*, pp. 287–89.

19. Kenyon, 2: 64; letter dated 7 April 1852.

20. Ibid., pp. 70, 76.

21. Ibid., p. 222.

22. Huxley, pp. 234, 236.

23. Kenyon, 2: 231.

24. For appreciative insights into the poem and for comments on Emily Dickinson's indebtedness to it see Ellen Moers, *Literary Women*, pp. 56–61.

25. Taplin, pp. 310–13.

26. William De Vane, *A Browning Handbook*, p. 207. De Vane quotes Hiram Corson, *Introduction to Browning*, p. 110,

as his source for identifying the lover as Sand. See also De Vane, *Shorter Poems of Robert Browning,* p. 315.

CHAPTER VII

1. Cross, *Life of George Eliot,* p. 3. Cross cites the wrong date; actually Sand went to the convent in 1817.

2. Published in the *Christian Observer* in January 1840. Cross quotes the poem in full, pp. 29–30.

3. Charles Hennell's *Inquiry Concerning the Origin of Christianity* was translated into German with a preface by Strauss. It was Hennell's sister to whom Eliot wrote many letters describing an indebtedness to Sand.

4. Haight, *Letters,* 2: 171.

5. J. Lewis May, *George Eliot,* pp. 58, 278–80.

6. Haight, *Letters,* 1: 203, 270, 275.

7. Ibid., p. 241.

8. Cross, p. 86. Moraud (p. 402) quotes this letter to Miss Hennell and assumes that the "letter about Lélia" is one that Eliot herself wrote but which Cross later suppressed. Haight (*Letters,* 1: 243) identifies the "letter" as the last of chapter 5 of Sand's *Lettres d'un Voyageur* (pp. 122–26 of the 1869 Paris edition), in which Sand defends *Lélia* against charges of immorality because of its truth to human experience.

9. Moraud, pp. 407, 400.

10. Haight, *Letters,* 1: 250–51.

11. Haight, *Letters,* 1: 267, 275.

12. Ibid., pp. 277–78. Haight identifies the "rushing mighty wind" as coming from Acts 2: 2 and the phrase "great power of God" as from Acts 8: 10. Joan Bennett (*George Eliot, Her Mind and Art,* p. 27) comments that all the "positives" in this appreciation of Sand's fiction apply to George Eliot's own.

13. Haight, *Letters,* 1: 278. Haight points out that the situation between the thirty-five-year-old Jacques and his seventeen-year-old bride has some resemblance to that between Casaubon and Dorothea in Eliot's *Middlemarch.* Haight also identifies the quotation, from part 1, letter 6, of *Jacques,* and gives the

quotation in the original. The *Foreign and Colonial* critic in 1843 gave the same quotation in translation in order to prove Sand a dangerous enemy to the institution of marriage. Walter Houghton (*Victorian Frame of Mind,* p. 364) quotes the speech —Sand's most devastating attack on marriage—as her "actual position."

14. Haight, *Letters,* 1: 254.

15. Ibid., p. 300. Dickens made a similar comment to Wilkie Collins in January 1856: "I met Madame Georges Sand the other day at a dinner got up by Madame Viardot for that great purpose. The human mind cannot conceive any one more astonishingly opposed to all my preconceptions. If I had been shown her in a state of repose, and asked what I thought her to be, I should have said: 'The Queen's monthly nurse.' *Au reste,* she has nothing of the *bas bleu* about her, and is very quiet and agreeable." G. Hogarth and M. Dickens, eds., *The Letters of Charles Dickens 1833–1856,* 1: 420–21.

16. Haight, *Letters,* 2: 67, 5, 31.

17. Ibid., 2: 91, 3: 374, 3: 416.

18. Lawrence and Elizabeth Hanson, *Marian Evans and George Eliot,* pp. 233, 234.

19. Haight, *Letters,* 5: 7.

20. Ibid., pp. 8–9. Haight identifies the picture as the Burton portrait of George Eliot. The picture of Sand is a pencil drawing done in 1850, now hanging in the Carnavalet Museum, and reproduced in *Bookman* 10 (1899): 305.

21. Winwar, p. 213.

22. Haight, *Letters,* 5: 464.

23. Ibid., 6: 312n.

24. "George Sand," *Temple Bar,* 73: 480–95.

25. *George Eliot,* p. 111; *Hours in a Library,* pp. 158–60.

26. Moraud, pp. 405, 400.

27. Haight, *Letters,* 2: 379.

28. Moraud, p. 396.

29. Elizabeth S. Haldane, *George Eliot and Her Times,* p. 301.

CHAPTER VIII

1. George W. E. Russell, ed., *Works of Matthew Arnold,* 14: 189. Russell identifies the book referred to as *A Memoir of the Rev. John Keble, M.A.* (1869) by Sir J. T. Coleridge.

2. Howard Foster Lowry, *The Letters of Matthew Arnold to Arthur Hugh Clough,* p. 20.

3. Ibid., pp. 44–45.

4. Ibid., pp. 58–59. Lionel Trilling points out that, as with Byron, Arnold never comments on Sand's sexual vagaries. Trilling states wryly that Arnold probably could not "impugn the morals of a lady he had visited"; or he simply felt her virtues outnumbered her vices. See Trilling, *Matthew Arnold,* p. 380.

5. Matthew Arnold, *Mixed Essays,* pp. 236–39.

6. Russell, *Letters,* 3: 14 (vol. 15 of *Works*); letter dated June 1876. Trilling comments that Sand may have meant nothing more than that Arnold was "English, handsome, conceited and on his travels." She may have meant, however, Trilling adds, that Arnold had the "gravity of a Milton and the unmistakable air of a self-dedicated man" (p. 16). This was Arnold's only visit, although George Saintsbury (p. 74) supposes that Arnold saw Sand a second time.

7. Iris Esther Sells, *Matthew Arnold and France,* pp. 28–36. Arnold did not visit Chamouni until later. In 1858 he wrote his sister: "It will be curious if I again miss Chamouni, which I have missed so often." Rain, however, prevented his going and it was not until the next year that he visited the place. As late as 1865 his enthusiasm for Sand remained high enough for him to attempt to visit the mountain monastery on Camaldoli, the site of Lélia's cell and famous for its view of Vesuvius and the Bay of Naples. Traveling as a commissioner on the continent, Arnold tried to get his driver to take him up the mountain, but the driver refused because of bad weather and its dangerous effect on the mountain road. Arnold wrote of his disappointment. Sells, pp. 24–25.

8. Frederick L. Mulhauser, *The Correspondence of Arthur*

Hugh Clough, 1: 178–79; letter to J. C. Sharp dated 22 February 1847.

9. Lowry, pp. 77–80 (see chap. 4 above), 133, 139.

10. Stuart P. Sherman, *Matthew Arnold,* p. 26.

11. Ibid., p. 27. Arnold identifies "fat old Muse" as the words of M. de Circourt.

12. Russell, *Letters,* 1: 140–41 (vol. 13 of *Works*).

13. Ibid., 3: 14 (vol. 15 of *Works*). This is the same letter to "Fan," in which Arnold related Sand's opinion of him, given by Renan to Morley.

14. Ibid., p. 22.

15. Ibid., p. 118.

16. Ibid., p. 334.

17. The first type is like Faust and Werther: exaltation of ambition or of passion, or the struggle of man with material things; Sand compares this type to the bird which dies in his cage. The second type is like Chateaubriand's René, who suffers because he has power or genius that he does not have the will to express; Sand compares this type to the eagle, which though wounded, beats its wings and resumes its flight. The third type is like Obermann, who has an intuition of definite but incomplete faculties; Sand compares this type to the bird which denied wings by nature issues a melancholy plaint as it sits on its reef. In the same preface Sand characterized Obermann as the "dream of powerlessness, the continuance of unformulated desire." The fourth type is like Lélia, one who suffers when his soul fails to realize its destiny, a destiny which eludes as in a dream. The will to act remains but power to act is gone and only desire remains. Sells, pp. 21–22.

18. Sells, p. 25.

19. Kenneth Allott, "Matthew Arnold's Reading Lists in Three Early Diaries," *Victorian Studies* 2: 257.

20. C. B. Tinker and H. F. Lowry, *Poetical Works of Matthew Arnold,* p. 498.

21. Written in November 1849 and first published in 1852. Sainte-Beuve admired the "Stanzas" so much that he translated

them into French prose; Arnold wrote him of the French version that he had never read his poem with so much pleasure. Tinker and Lowry, *A Commentary,* p. 261.

22. First published in 1867, it bears an epitaph from Obermann: "Savez-vous quelque bien qui console du regret d'un monde?" Tinker and Lowry, *Poetical Works of Matthew Arnold,* p. 312. Tinker and Lowry comment that a better quotation would be this from Sénancour entered in the *Note-Books* in 1866: "mais la tendance à l'ordre ne peut-elle faire une partie essentielle de nos inclinations, de notre instinct, comme la tendance à la conservation, à la reproduction." Tinker and Lowry, *A Commentary,* pp. 264–65. Quoted from "Obermann Once More" are lines 280–84 and 320–24.

23. As Tinker and Lowry put it: "Arnold's stoicism had always been a little more exhilarating and highly-coloured than stoicism ought to be. The powerful spirit of Dr. Arnold was forever dealing with René and his like, and making even Epictetus and Marcus Aurelius greater than they knew" (*A Commentary,* p. 262).

24. Ibid., p. 273.

25. Fraser Neiman, ed., *Essays, Letters, and Reviews by Matthew Arnold,* p. 159.

26. Trilling, p. 381.

27. Ibid., pp. 128n, 381–82.

28. Arnold, *Mixed Essays,* pp. 240–60. Published in *Nineteenth Century* 1 (April 1879): 221–41.

29. Curtis Cate in his biography *George Sand* thinks Arnold chose this novel because in it she struck an antiromantic note, attacking morbid introspection and recommending a study of nature as therapy for lovesick souls. Certainly in his 1853 preface Arnold attacked the dramatic dialogue of the mind with itself; yet he wrote Clough earlier that he liked the "scenery bits," the nature scenes, which would be Wordsworthian, not antiromantic.

30. Arnold, *Works,* 4: 245.

31. Ibid., 4: 146–47.

32. Ibid., 16: 272.

33. Ibid., 1: 312.

34. Ibid., 4: 248. Arnold had been a bad prophet before when he compared Joubert to Coleridge. See "Joubert a French Coleridge."

35. Ibid., p. 249.

36. George Saintsbury, *Matthew Arnold,* p. 181; Herbert Paul, *Matthew Arnold,* pp. 82–83.

37. E. K. Brown, *Matthew Arnold, A Study in Conflict,* p. 98.

38. Ibid., p. 113. Brown refers to Lewis Gates's four categories of Arnold's style: (1) the severe, exact style of education reports; (2) the familiar, easy style of literary essays and of the blander parts of his social criticism, (3) the no less familiar, but harsher style when he discusses a topic that arouses the evangelist in him, and (4) the emotional highly wrought style of a few passages and of a number of passages when he is paying tribute to someone who, like George Sand, had helped to form his youth. Brown, p. 10.

39. Lowry, Young, and Dunn, *The Note-Books of Matthew Arnold,* pp. 8, 14, 24, 30, 34, 47, 439, 484, and 485.

40. Ibid., p. 2.

41. Ibid., p. 8.

42. Ibid., pp. 10–11.

43. Ibid., p. 59.

44. Ibid., p. 277.

45. Ibid., p. 383.

46. Ibid., p. 410.

47. Ibid., pp. 494–95.

48. Ibid., p. 523.

CHAPTER IX

1. See John Holloway, *Victorian Sage* (New York: W. W. Norton and Co., 1953). A good summary of the tendency is described by Walter Houghton, *Victorian Frame of Mind,* pp. 99 ff.

2. *The Moonstone,* p. 3.

3. This thesis is developed in Walter Jackson Bate's essay

"Matthew Arnold" in *Criticism: The Major Texts* (New York: Harcourt, Brace and Co., 1952).

4. "Memorial Verses," ll. 8–11.

5. Frederic W. H. Myers, *Nineteenth Century* 1: 229.

6. *Foreign and Colonial Quarterly Review* 1: 479.

7. Joseph Barry, *Infamous Woman,* p. 143.

8. Praz, *The Romantic Agony,* p. 333.

9. Susanne Howe, *Geraldine Jewsbury,* p. 54. Virginia Woolf explores this friendship in her essay "Geraldine and Jane," in the *Common Reader,* second series, pp. 85–201. A recent study of the author of Sherlock Holmes by Samuel Rosenberg states that fiction is the working out of a frustrated homosexuality and that Irene Adler, the emancipated woman in the Holmes stories, is George Sand. See Rosenberg, *Naked Is the Best Disguise,* pp. 2, 102.

10. See Cate, p. 228.

11. Winwar, pp. 273–74.

12. In *Enemy of the People,* Act 4, Dr. Stockmann says: "The majority *never* has right on its side. . . . This is one of those social lies against which an independent, intelligent man must wage war."

13. Bolton King, *Life and Writings of Joseph Mazzini,* pp. 90–92.

14. George Sand, *Lélia,* translated with an introduction by Maria Espinosa (Bloomington: Indiana University Press, 1978).

APPENDIX

Translations of George Sand's Works Available 1847–1902

Biographies of Sand say little about translations of her novels. Likewise there is not much information concerning such translations in letters written by Victorians or in the periodical reviews of the time. The *Quarterly Review* in 1847 criticized a proposed translation of Sand's works by "an English editrix" and the Reverend E. R. Larkin. The editrix was Matilda Hays, whose six-volume edition of Sand's works was published by Churton in 1847. Joseph Mazzini wrote a preface for Eliza Ashurst's translation of Sand's *Letters of a Traveller*. (The source for this statement is *Life and Writings of Mazzini*, 6: 32. Neither the *British Museum Catalogue* nor the *English Catalogue of Books* lists the translation, nor do the biographies by Stringfellow Barr and Edyth Hinkley refer to it. The *Catalogue of the London Library* lists a critical review of Sand by Mazzini in a translation of *Little Fadette* in 1850.)

In 1853 Elizabeth Barrett Browning wrote that in Rome she had met both Matilda Hays and Eliza Ashurst, whom she identified as translators of Sand. George Eliot in 1861 from Florence wrote to John Blackwood, suggesting as a possible translator for her *Scenes of Clerical Life* a "Mrs. Blackwell"—Anna Blackwell, whose translations of Sand's *Jacques* had appeared in 1847.

Many translations appeared, and Victorians who could not read Sand in the original French could read her in a variety of translations. The following is a partial list of the translations published between 1847 and 1902, arranged alphabetically by title, then arranged chronologically for each translation. The items are taken from *The British Museum General Catalogue of Printed Books* photolithographic edition to 1955, volume 212

(London, 1964) and the *Five Years Supplement,* volume 21 (London, 1972); from the *English Catalogue of Books* (London, 1863, 1873, 1882, 1889, 1898, 1898–1900), volumes 1–6; and from *Catalogue of the London Library* (London, 1914), volume 2. The dates in brackets are dates of publication of the first editions in French.

André [1835]

1847: Churton. In vol. 1 of *Works.* Translated by Matilda M. Hays.

Antonia [1863]

1870: no imprint (Boston). Translated by V. Vaughan.

Bagpipers [1853]

1890: Roberts Brothers (Boston). Translated by K. P. Wormeley.

The Castle of Pictordu [1872]

1884: Gemmell (Edinburgh); Simpkin (London). Translated by Georgina S. Grahame.

Césarine Dietrich [1870]

1871: no imprint (Boston). Translated by E. Stanwood.

Companion of the Tour of France [1841]

1847: Churton. As vol. 2 of *Works.* Translated by Matilda M. Hays.

1849: J. M'Glashan (Dublin). As *Journeyman Joiner or Companion of the Tour of France.* Translated by F. G. Shaw.

1849: Tegg. As *Journeyman Joiner or Companion of the Tour of France.* Translator unknown.

Consuelo [1842]

1847: Parlour Library. 2 vols. Translator unknown.

1847: no imprint (Boston). 3 vols. Translated by F. G. Shaw.

1851: no imprint (New York). Translated by Fayette Robinson.

1858: T. Hodgson. Translator unknown.

1876: Weldon. Translator unknown.
1894: W. Scott. Translated by Fayette Robinson.

The Countess of Rudolstadt [1844]

1847: Parlour Library. Translator unknown.
1847: no imprint (Boston). Translated by F. G. Shaw.
1862: Shilling Readable Novels. Translator unknown.
1863: C. H. Clarke. Translator unknown.
1878: Weldon. Translator unknown.
1893: Oxford Library. Translated by Fayette Robinson.
1895: W. Scott. Translated by Fayette Robinson.

Devil's Pool [1846]

1848: Parlour Library. As *Haunted Marsh*. Translator unknown.
1850: Slater. As *Enchanted Lake*. Translated by F. G. Shaw.
1861: Lea. Translator unknown.
1895: Dent. Translated by Jane M. Sedgwick and Ellen Sedgwick.

François the Waif [1847]

1888: no imprint. As *Episodes from François le Champi*, ed. with notes by C. Sankey. Translator unknown.
1889: Routledge. Translated by G. Masson.
1895: Dent. Translated by Jane Minto Sedgwick.

Impressions and Reminiscences [1862]

1874: R. H. Stoddard. As *Recollections by George Sand [Selected Passages trans. from "Impressions et Souvenirs"]*. Bric-à-Brac Series, vol. 3.
1877: no imprint (Boston). Translated by H. K. Adams.

Jacques [1834]

1847: no imprint (New York). Translated by Anna Blackwell.

Lady Blake's Love Letters, etc.
Trans. from French of George Sand's Lavinia

1884: no imprint. Translated by Page McCarty.

Last of Aldini [1839]

1847: Churton. In vol. 3 of *Works*. Translated by Matilda M. Hays.

A Letter to M. Régnier . . . by George Sand, upon her adaptation to the French Stage of Shakespeare's "As You Like It" [1856]

1856: no imprint (London). Translated by Theodosia Lady Monson.

Letters of a Traveller [1837]

1847: Churton. As vol. 4 of *Works*. Translated by Matilda M. Hays.

L'Orco [1841]

1847: Churton. In vol. 1 of *Works*. Translated by Matilda M. Hays.

Letters of George Sand

1885: Ward and Downey. Vol. 1. Translated by R. Ledos de Beaufort.

1886: Ward and Downey. 3 vols. Translated by R. Ledos de Beaufort.

Little Fadette [1849]

1849: Slater. Translator unknown.

1850: no imprint (London). As *Little Fadette, a Domestic Story,* with analytic review of the life and writings of the author by Joseph Mazzini. Translator unknown.

1878: Weldon. As *Little Fadette, a Domestic Story*. Translator unknown.

1878: no imprint. As *Little Cricket. A Domestic Drama* adapted from a Pastoral Romance of George Sand [*La Petite Fadette*]. Translator unknown.

1885: no imprint. As *Fanchon the Cricket*. From a Tale of George Sand [*La Petite Fadette*]. Translator unknown.

1892: Percival. As *Petite Fadette*. Translated by F. A. Binas.

1895: Dent. As *Fadette*. Translated by Jane Minot Sedgwick. [First published in New York in 1893].

Mlle. Merquem

1868: no imprint (New York). Translator unknown.

The Marquis de Villemer [1860]

1871: no imprint (Boston). Translated by R. Keeler.

Mauprat [1837]

1847: Churton. As vol. 5 of *Works*. Translated by Matilda M. Hays.
1870: no imprint (Boston). Translated by V. Vaughan.
1878: Weldon. Translator unknown.
1891: Laird and Lee (Chicago). Translated by H. E. Miller.
1902: Heinemann. Translated by Stanley Young.

The Miller of Angibault [1845]

1847: Churton. As vol. 6 of *Works*. Translated by Matilda M. Hays.
1853: Simms. Translator unknown.
1878: Weldon. Translator unknown.

Mosaic Workers [1838]

1844: H. G. Clarke. Translated by E[liza] A. A[shurst].
1847: Churton. As *Mosaic Masters*, in vol. 1 of *Works*. Translated by Matilda M. Hays.
1895: Dent. As *Master Mosaic Workers*. Translated by Charlotte C. Johnston.
1900: Dent. As *Master Mosaic Workers*. Translated by Charlotte C. Johnston. Temple Classics for Young People.

My Sister Jeannie [1844]

1874: no imprint (Boston). Translated by S. R. Croker.
1878: Weldon. Translator unknown.

A Rolling Stone [1870]

1871: no imprint (Boston). Translated by C. Owen.

Simon [1836]

1847: Churton. In vol. 3 of *Works*. Translated by Matilda M. Hays.

The Snow Man, A Novel [1858]

1871: no imprint (Boston). Translated by V. Vaughan.

Spiridion [1839]

1842: Fox. Translator unknown.

Teverino [1845]

1855: no imprint (New York). Translated by "a Lady."

1870: no imprint (Philadelphia). As *Jealousy, or, Teverino*. Translator unknown.

Tower of Percemont and Marianne [1876]

1877: no imprint (New York). *Tower of Percemont*. Translator unknown.

1881: Vizetelly, Popular French Novels. Translator unknown. [First published in New York in 1877.]

The Uscoque, A Venetian Story [1838]

1850: Slater. Translated by J. S. Bauer.

The Wings of Courage and The Cloud Spinner, Two Stories [1873]

1883: Blackie and Son. Translated by Mrs. Cockran.

Bibliography

I. PRIMARY SOURCES

"The Abbé de la Mennais." *Foreign Quarterly Review* 21 (1838): 65–72 (Am. ed.).

"Alfred de Musset." *North British Review* 98 (1868): 154–59.

Allott, Kenneth. "Matthew Arnold's Reading Lists in Three Early Diaries." *Victorian Studies* 2 (1959): 254–66.

Arnold, Matthew. "Copyright." *Fortnightly Review* 27 (1880): 319–34.

———. *England and the Italian Question.* Edited by Merle Bevington. Durham: Duke University Press, 1953.

———. "George Sand." *Mixed Essays.* New York: Macmillan Co., 1901.

———. "Numbers." *Discourses in America.* London: Macmillan and Co., 1885.

———. *Works.* 15 vols. London: Macmillan and Co., 1903–1904.

Blessington, Countess of. *Idler in France.* 2 vols. London: H. Colburn, 1842.

Bowler, Victor E. A. "George Sand and Geraldine Jewsbury, An Unpublished Letter." *Revue de Littérature Comparée* 30 (1956): 396–98.

Brimley, George. *Essays.* London: Macmillan and Co., 1882.

Browning, Elizabeth Barrett. *The Complete Works.* Edited by Charlotte Porter and Helen A. Clarke. 6 vols. New York: Crowell, 1900.

[Busk, Mary Margaret Blair]. "George Sand's Novels." *Foreign Quarterly Review* 14 (1834): 143–57 (Am. ed.).

"Consuelo." *Foreign Quarterly Review* 31 (1843): 226–34 (Am. ed.).

"Contemporary Literature." *Westminster Review* 63 (1855): 311–14 (Am. ed.).

"The Countess Hahn-Hahn's Writings." *Edinburgh Review* 78 (1844): 81–98 (Am. ed.).

"Country Life." *Blackwood's Edinburgh Review* 120 (1876): 483–508.

[Croker, J. W.]. "French Novels." *Quarterly Review* 56 (1836): 65–131.

[Eastlake, Lady]. "Lady Travellers." *Quarterly Review* 76 (1845): 98–137.

[Eliot, George]. "Silly Novels by Lady Novelists." *Westminster Review* 66 (1856): 243ff.

"Employment of Women." *Dublin Review* 52 (1862): 1–44.

Espinasse, Francis. *Literary Recollections*. New York: Dodd, Mead, 1893.

"French Criticism of English Writers." *Foreign Quarterly Review* 30 (1842): 1–7.

"French Literature, Recent Novelists." *Edinburgh Review* 57 (1833): 330–57 (Am. ed.).

"French Novelists, No. 2. Georges Sand." *London Society* 21 (1872): 146–57.

"Genius of George Sand." *Bentley's Miscellany* 27 (1850): 506–13.

"George Sand." *Bentley's Quarterly Review* 2 (1859–1860): 369–403.

"George Sand." *Howitt's Journal of Literature and Popular Progress* 1 (1847): 128–30.

"George Sand." *Saturday Review* 14 (1862): 193–94.

"George Sand." *Sharpe's London Magazine of Entertainment and Instruction, Incorporated with the Illustrated Magazine* 37 (n.d.): 15–28.

"George Sand." *Temple Bar, Incorporated with Bentley's Miscellany* 72 (1885): 480–95.

Goethe, Johann Wolfgang von. *Faust*. Translated by Louis MacNiece. London: Oxford University Press, 1951.

"Histoire de ma Vie—Par George Sand." *London Quarterly Review* 143 (1887): 221–35.

"History of Frederick II of Prussia." *Dublin Review* 47 (1859): 132–68.

"History of Frederick II of Prussia." *Dublin Review* 51 (1862): 404–28.

"Horace." *Foreign Quarterly Review* 24 (1842): 289–91 (Am. ed.).

James, Henry. "George Sand." *Galaxy* 24 (1877): 45–61.

Kennedy, Patrick. "The Life, Eccentricities, and Literature of George Sand." *Dublin University Magazine* 61 (1863): 220–33.

"La Petite Fadette." *Blackwood's Edinburgh Review* 66 (1849): 607–19.

"Letters and Impressions from Paris." *Blackwood's Edinburgh Magazine* 60 (1846): 423–25.

[Lewes, George Henry]. "Complete Works of George Sand." *Foreign Quarterly Review* 32 (1844): 145–63 (Am. ed.).

———. "George Sand's Recent Novels." *Foreign Quarterly Review* 37 (1846): 12–20.

———. "Lady Novelists." *Westminster Review* 58 (1852): 70–77.

———. "The New Classic Drama in France." *Foreign Quarterly Review* 36 (1846): 18–22 (Am. ed.).

"Life and Writings of Sainte-Beuve." *London Quarterly Review* 141 (1876): 89–110.

"Literary Notices." *Wesleyan Methodist* 78 (1855): 73.

"Literary Tendencies in France." *North British Review* 50 (1856): 188–202.

"Living English Poets." *Dublin Review* 69 (1861): 503–42.

"M. de Chateaubriand." *North British Review* 57 (1858): 1–14.

"The Macaulay Election of 1846, Containing Comments on the Macaulay Rejection of 1847." *Quarterly Review* 81 (1847): 526–40.

Masson, Gustave. "On Romanticism and on the Present State of French Literature." *Wesleyan Methodist* 70 (1847): 35–39.

[Mazzini, Joseph]. "George Sand." *Monthly Chronicle* 4 (1839): 23–40.

Mazzini, Joseph. "George Sand." *The People's Journal* 3 (1847): 131–34.

———. *Life and Writings of Joseph Mazzini*. 6 vols. London: Smith, Elder, 1891.

[Mazzini, Joseph]. "The Present State of French Literature." *Monthly Chronicle* 3 (1839): 217–25.

"Memoirs of the Countess Maria Aurora of Königsmark from Sources Hitherto Unknown." *Foreign Quarterly Review* 18 (1837): 50–57 (Am. ed.).

"Modern French Literature." *Edinburgh Review* 101 (1855): 48–62 (Am. ed.).

"Modern French Literature of France." *Eclectic Review* 8 (1840): 534–47.

Monod, G. "Contemporary Life and Thought." *Contemporary Review* 21 (1878): 391–421.

"Munch's Studies and Recollections." *Foreign Quarterly Review* 20 (1838): 176–86.

Myers, Frederic W. H. "George Sand." *Nineteenth Century* 1 (1877): 221–41.

"Oeuvres Complètes de George Sand." *Foreign and Colonial Quarterly Review* 1 (1843): 478–508.

[Oliphant, Mrs. M.O.W.]. "Alfred de Musset." *Blackwood's Edinburgh Magazine* 120 (1876): 361–82.

———. "Two Cities—Two Books." *Blackwood's Edinburgh Magazine* 116 (1874): 72–91.

"Parcel from Paris." *Blackwood's Edinburgh Magazine* 64 (1848): 557–72.

"Prince Talleyrand." *Blackwood's Edinburgh Magazine* 37 (1835): 76–81.

"The Quarterly Review for April, 1836. Article on French Novels." *London and Westminster Review* 3 and 25 (1836): 167–73 (Am. ed.).

"Rousseau's Nouvelle Héloïse and the Modern Literature Extravagant." *Foreign Quarterly Review* 27 (1841): 63–76 (Am. ed.).

Sand, George. *Consuelo*. The Masterpieces of George Sand,

vols. 2–4. Translated by G. Burnham Ives. Philadelphia: Barrie and Sons, 1900.

———. *The Devil's Pool.* Translated by Hamish Miles. London: Scholartis Press, 1929.

———. *Francis the Waif.* Translated by Gustave Masson. London: G. Routledge and Sons, 1889.

———. *Histoire de ma Vie.* 5 vols. Paris: M. Levy, 1856.

———. *Indiana.* Masterpieces of George Sand, vol. 1. Translated by G. Burnham Ives. Philadelphia: G. Barrie and Sons, 1900.

———. *Lélia,* rev. ed., Paris: Calmann Levy, 1881.

———. *Les Maîtres Mosaïstes,* Paris: M. Levy, 1869.

———. *Little Fadette.* Translated by Hamish Miles. London: Scholartis Press, 1928.

———. *Marquis de Villemer.* The Masterpieces of George Sand, vol. 18. Translated by G. Burnham Ives. Philadelphia: G. Barrie and Sons, 1900.

———. *Mauprat.* Translated by Stanley Young. New York: D. Appleton and Co., 1902.

———. *She and He.* The Masterpieces of George Sand, vol. 20. Translated by G. Burnham Ives. Philadelphia: G. Barrie and Sons, 1900.

———. *Sin of Monsieur Antoine.* The Masterpieces of George Sand, vols. 5–6. Translated by G. Burnham Ives. Philadelphia: G. Barrie and Sons, 1900.

———. *Valentine.* The Masterpieces of George Sand, vol. 18. Translated by G. Burnham Ives. Philadelphia: G. Barrie and Sons, 1900.

[Sandars, T. C.]. "Histoire de ma Vie and Oeuvres de George Sand." *National Review* 6 (1858): 37–69.

[Shand, A. Innes]. "George Sand." *Blackwood's Edinburgh Magazine* 121 (1877): 70–93.

"Spindler's Novels—The Natural Son." *Edinburgh Review* 61 (1835): 37–42 (Am. ed.).

[Thackeray, William]. "Balzac on the Newspapers of Paris." *Foreign Quarterly Review* 31 (1843): 99–103 (Am. ed.).

Thackeray, William. *The Paris Sketch Book of Mr. M. A. Titmarsh*. New York: John W. Lovell Co., 1883.

"*The Victims of Society* by Lady Blessington." *Edinburgh Review* 67 (1838): 186–90 (Am. ed.).

"Weber's Life of Marshal Saxe." *Edinburgh Review* 120 (1864): 259–77 (Am. ed.).

"A Winter in South of Europe." *Athenaeum* 723 (1841): 687–89.

"The Works of George Sand." *British and Foreign Review* 8 (1839): 360–90.

II. SECONDARY SOURCES

Ashley, Robert. *Wilkie Collins*. New York: Roy Publishers, 1952.

Bain, Alexander. *John Stuart Mill*. London: Longmans, Green and Co., 1882.

Barr, Stringfellow. *Mazzini: Portrait of an Exile*. New York: H. Holt and Co., 1935.

Barry, Joseph. *Infamous Woman: The Life of George Sand*. New York: Doubleday and Co., 1977.

Bennett, Joan. *George Eliot, Her Mind and Art*. Cambridge: Cambridge University Press, 1948.

Bevington, Merle Mowbray. *The Saturday Review, 1855–1888*. New York: Columbia University Press, 1941.

Bibliographie de la Littérature Française de 1800 à 1930. Edited by Hugo P. Thieme. Vol. 2. Paris: Librarie E. Droz, 1933.

Bigland, Eileen. *Ouida: The Passionate Victorian*. New York: Duell, Sloan and Pearce, 1951.

Bliss, Trudy, ed. *Jane Welsh Carlyle: A New Selection of Her Letters*. London: Victor Gollancz, 1949.

———, ed. *Thomas Carlyle: Letters to His Wife*. London: Victor Gollancz, 1953.

Brightfield, Myron F. *John Wilson Croker*. Berkeley: University of California Press, 1940.

British Museum General Catalogue of Printed Books. Vol. 212.

London: Trustees of the British Museum, 1964. *Five Year Supplement*. Vol. 21. London, 1972.

Brown, E. K. *Matthew Arnold: A Study in Conflict*. Chicago: University of Chicago Press, 1948.

Brown, Horatio F. *John Addington Symonds*. London: Nimmo, 1903.

Carlyle, Alexander, ed. *Letters of Thomas Carlyle to John Stuart Mill, John Sterling, and Robert Browning*. New York: Frederick A. Stokes Co., 1923.

———, ed. *Love Letters of Thomas Carlyle and Jane Welsh*. 2 vols. London: John Lane, 1909.

———, ed. *New Letters of Thomas Carlyle*. 2 vols. London: J. Lane, 1904.

Caro, Elme Marie. *George Sand*. Paris: Hachette, 1887.

Catalogue Général des Livres Imprimés de la Bibliothèque Nationale. Paris: Bibliothèque Nationale, 1941.

Catalogue of the London Library. Vol. 2. London, 1914.

Cate, Curtis. *George Sand, a Biography*. Boston: Houghton Mifflin Co., 1975.

Chambers, E. K. *Matthew Arnold: A Study*. London: Oxford University Press, 1947.

Clive, John. *Scotch Reviewers: The Edinburgh Review, 1802–1815*. Cambridge: Harvard University Press, 1957.

Cross, J. W. *Life of George Eliot*. New York: Harper and Brothers, 1885.

Cross, Wilbur. *The Development of the English Novel*. New York: Macmillan Co., 1926.

Cruse, Amy. *The Englishman and His Books in the Early Nineteenth Century*. London: G. G. Harrap and Co., 1930.

Curran, Eileen. "*The Foreign Quarterly Review* (1827–1846): A British Interpretation of Modern Literature." Ph.D. dissertation, Cornell University, 1958.

David, Nuel Pharr. *The Life of Wilkie Collins*. Urbana: University of Illinois Press, 1956.

Decker, Clarence R. *The Victorian Conscience*. New York: Twayne, 1952.

De Selincourt, Ernest. *The Letters of William and Dorothy Wordsworth: The Later Years.* 3 vols. Oxford: Clarendon Press, 1939.

DeVane, William C. *A Browning Handbook.* New York: F. S. Crofts and Co., 1940.

———. *Shorter Poems of Robert Browning.* New York: F. S. Crofts and Co., 1934.

Doumic, René. *George Sand: Some Aspects of Her Life.* Translated by Alys Hallard. New York: G. P. Putnam's Sons, 1910.

"Editions Originales de George Sand." *Biblio* 20 (1954): 12–13.

Edwards, Samuel. *George Sand: A Biography of the First Modern Liberated Woman.* New York: David McKay, 1972.

English Catalogue of Books. Vols. 1–6. London: Publisher's Circular, 1863–98.

Everett, Edwin Mallard. *The Party of Humanity: The Fortnightly Review and Its Contributors, 1865–1874.* Chapel Hill: University of North Carolina Press, 1939.

Ffrench, Yvonne. *Ouida: A Study in Ostentation.* London: Cobden-Sanderson, 1938.

Ford, George H. *Dickens and His Readers.* Princeton: Published for the University of Cincinnati by Princeton University Press, 1955.

Froude, J. A. *Letters and Memorials of Jane Welsh Carlyle.* 2 vols. New York: Harper and Brothers, 1883.

Gaskell, Mrs. E. C. *The Life of Charlotte Brontë.* London: J. M. Dent and Co., 1908.

Goodwin, Michael. *Nineteenth-Century Opinion.* London: Penguin Books, 1951.

Graham, Walter. *English Literary Periodicals.* New York: T. Nelson and Sons, 1930.

———. *Tory Criticism in the Quarterly Review.* New York: Columbia University Press, 1921.

Gribble, Francis. *George Sand and Her Lovers.* New York: E. P. Dutton and Co., 1976.

Haight, Gordon S. *George Eliot and John Chapman.* New Haven: Yale University Press, 1940.

Haight, Gordon S., ed. *The George Eliot Letters*. 7 vols. New Haven: Yale University Press, 1954.

Haldane, Elizabeth S. *George Eliot and Her Times: A Victorian Study*. New York: D. Appleton and Co., 1927.

———. *Mrs. Gaskell and Her Friends*. London: Hodder and Stoughton, 1931.

Halliday, J. L. *Mr. Carlyle My Patient: A Psychosomatic Biography*. London: Heinemann, 1949.

Hanson, Lawrence and Elisabeth. *Marian Evans and George Eliot*. London: Oxford University Press, 1952.

———. *Necessary Evil: The Life of Jane Welsh Carlyle*. New York: Macmillan Co., 1952.

Harvey, Charles H. *Matthew Arnold*. London: J. Clarke and Co., 1931.

Hayek, F. A. *John Stuart Mill and Harriet Taylor*. Chicago: University of Chicago Press, 1951.

Hewlett, Dorothy. *Elizabeth Barrett Browning*. New York: Knopf, 1952.

Hinkley, Edyth. *Mazzini*. London: Putnam, 1924.

Hogarth, G., and Dickens M., eds. *Letters of Charles Dickens, 1833–1856*. 2 vols. London: Chapman and Hall, 1880.

Hood, Thurman L., ed. *Letters of Robert Browning*. Collected by Thomas J. Wise. New Haven: Yale University Press, 1933.

Houghton, Walter E. *The Victorian Frame of Mind 1830–1870*. New Haven: Yale University Press, 1957.

Howe, Cliff, ed. *Lovers and Libertines*. New York: Ace Books, 1958.

Howe, Marie Jenny. *George Sand: The Search for Love*. New York: John Day Co., 1927.

Howe, Susanne. *Geraldine Jewsbury: Her Life and Errors*. London: G. Allen and Unwin, 1935.

Hutton, Lawrence, ed. *Letters of Charles Dickens to Wilkie Collins*. New York: Harper and Brothers, 1892.

Huxley, Leonard, ed. *Elizabeth Barrett Browning: Letters to Her Sister, 1846–1859*. London: J. Murray, 1929.

———. *Jane Welsh Carlyle: Letters to Her Family, 1839–1863*. New York: J. Murray, 1924.

Johnson, Diane. *Lesser Lives*. New York: Knopf, 1972.

Johnson, R. Brimley. *The Letters of George Eliot*. London: J. Lane, 1926.

Karenine, Vladimir. *George Sand: Sa Vie et ses Oeuvres*. Paris: P. Ollendorff, 1889.

Kenyon, Frederic G., ed. *Letters of Elizabeth Barrett Browning*. 2 vols. New York: Macmillan Co., 1899.

King, Bolton, ed. *Mazzini's Letters*. Translated by Alice de Rosen Jervis. London: J. M. Dent and Sons, 1930.

———. *Life of Mazzini*. London: J. M. Dent and Co., 1902.

Landis, Paul, and Freeman, Ronald E., eds. *Letters of the Brownings to George Barrett*. Urbana: University of Illinois Press, 1958.

Lee, Elizabeth. *Ouida: A Memoir*. London: T. F. Unwin, 1914.

Lowry, Howard Foster, ed. *The Letters of Matthew Arnold to Arthur Hugh Clough*. New York: Oxford University Press, 1932.

———; Young, Karl; and Dunn, Waldo Hilary, eds. *The Note-Books of Matthew Arnold*. London: Oxford University Press, 1952.

Maitland, Frederic William. *The Life and Letters of Leslie Stephen*. London: Duckworth and Co., 1906.

Marchand, Leslie A. *The Athenaeum: A Mirror of Victorian Culture*. Chapel Hill: University of North Carolina Press, 1941.

Marriott, Sir John Arthur Ransome. *The Makers of Modern Italy*. London: Macmillan and Co., 1889.

Maurois, André. *Lélia: The Life of George Sand*. Translated by Gerard Hopkins. New York: Harper, 1953.

May, J. Lewis. *George Eliot*. London: Cassell, 1930.

Meredith, George. *Letters of George Meredith*. Edited by his son. New York: Charles Scribner's Sons, 1912.

Miller, Betty, ed. *Elizabeth Barrett to Miss Mitford*. London: John Murray, 1954.

Mineka, Francis E. *The Dissidence of Dissent: The Monthly Repository 1806–1838*. Chapel Hill: University of North Carolina Press, 1944.

Mineka, Francis E., ed. *The Earlier Letters of John Stuart Mill 1812–1848*. Collected Works of John Stuart Mill, vols. 12 and 13. Toronto: University of Toronto Press, 1963.

Moers, Ellen. *Literary Women*. New York: Doubleday and Co., 1973.

Moraud, Marcel. *Le Romantisme Français en Angleterre de 1814 à 1848*. Paris: H. Champion, 1933.

Morley, John. *Critical Miscellanies*. 3 vols. London: Macmillan and Co., 1886.

Mueller, Iris Wessel. *John Stuart Mill and French Thought*. Urbana: University of Illinois Press, 1956.

Mulhauser, Frederick L. *The Correspondence of Arthur Hugh Clough*. Oxford: Clarendon Press, 1957.

Neiman, Fraser. *Essays, Letters and Reviews by Matthew Arnold*. Cambridge: Harvard University Press, 1960.

Nesbitt, George L. *Benthamite Reviewing: The First Twelve Years of the Westminster Review 1824–1836*. New York: Columbia University Press, 1934.

Nietzsche, Friedrich Wilhelm. "Skirmishes of an Untimely Man." *Twilight of the Idols. Portable Nietzsche,* edited by Walter Kaufman. New York: Viking Press, 1954.

Norton, Charles Eliot. *Letters of Thomas Carlyle 1826–1836*. London: Macmillan and Co., 1889.

———. *Reminiscences by Thomas Carlyle*. 2 vols. London and Toronto: J. M. Dent and Sons, 1932.

Oliphant, Mrs. M.O.W. *The Autobiography and Letters of Mrs. M.O.W. Oliphant*. New York: Dodd, Mead and Co., 1899.

Packe, Michael St. John. *The Life of John Stuart Mill*. New York: Macmillan Co., 1954.

Pailleron, Marie Louise. *George Sand: Histoire de sa Vie*. 3 vols. Paris: B. Grasset, 1938–1953.

Pankhurst, Richard K. P. *The Saint Simonians, Mill and Carlyle*. London: Sidgwick and Jackson, 1957.

Paterson, Arthur. *George Eliot's Family Life and Letters*. London: Selwyn and Blount, 1928.

Paul, Herbert. *Matthew Arnold*. English Men of Letters Series. New York: Macmillan Co., 1903.

Pearl, Cyril. *The Girl with the Swansdown Seat*. Indianapolis: Bobbs-Merrill, 1955.

Praz, Mario. *The Romantic Agony*. New York: Oxford University Press, 1970.

Romieu, Emilie and Georges. *The Life of George Eliot*. Translated by Brian W. Downs. London: J. Cape, 1932.

Rosenberg, Samuel. *Naked is the Best Disguise*. Indianapolis: Bobbs-Merrill, 1974.

Rossi, Joseph. *The Image of America in Mazzini's Writings*. Madison: University of Wisconsin Press, 1954.

Rudman, Harry. *Italian Nationalism and English Letters*. New York: Columbia University Press, 1940.

Ruskin, John. *The Complete Works of John Ruskin*. Edited by E. T. Cook and Alexander Wedderburn. 39 vols. London: G. Allen, 1904–1912.

Saintsbury, George. *Matthew Arnold*. New York: Dodd, Mead and Co., 1909.

Schermerhorn, Elizabeth. *The Seven Strings of the Lyre: The Romantic Life of George Sand*. New York: Houghton Mifflin Co., 1927.

Scudder, Townsend. *Jane Welsh Carlyle*. New York: Macmillan Co., 1939.

Sells, Iris Esther. *Matthew Arnold and France*. Cambridge: At the University Press, 1935.

Sencourt, Robert E. *The Life of George Meredith*. New York: Scribners, 1929.

Seyd, Felizia. *Romantic Rebel: The Life and Times of George Sand*. New York: Viking Press, 1940.

Shephard, Esther. *Walt Whitman's Pose*. New York: Harcourt, Brace and Co., 1938.

Sherman, Stuart P. *Matthew Arnold How to Know Him*. Indianapolis: Bobbs-Merrill Co., 1917.

———. *The George Sand—Gustave Flaubert Letters*. Translated by Aimee L. McKenzie. London: Duckworth and Co., 1922.

Shine, Hill, and Shine, Helen Chadwick. *The Quarterly Review Under Gifford: Identification of Contributors 1809–1824*. Chapel Hill: University of North Carolina Press, 1949.

Sleumer, Albert. *Index Romanus*. Osnabruck: J. Jouscher, 1956.

Stephen, Leslie. *George Eliot*. English Men of Letters Series. New York: Macmillan Co., 1902.

———. *Hours in a Library*. London: G. Putnam's Sons, 1904.

Tannenbaum, S. A. *John Ford, Thomas Nash, Two Concise Bibliographies*. New York: S. A. Tannenbaum, 1941.

Taplin, Gardner B. *The Life of Elizabeth Barrett Browning*. New Haven: Yale University Press, 1957.

Thomas, Bertha. *George Sand*. Boston: Roberts Brothers, 1883.

Thomson, Patricia. *George Sand and the Victorians*. New York: Columbia University Press, 1977.

Tillotson, Kathleen. *Novels of the Eighteen-Forties*. Oxford: Clarendon Press, 1954.

Tinker, C. B., and Lowry, H. F. *The Poetical Works of Matthew Arnold*. New York: Oxford University Press, 1950.

———. *The Poetry of Matthew Arnold: A Commentary*. London: Oxford University Press, 1940.

Trilling, Lionel. *Matthew Arnold*. New York: W. W. Norton and Co., 1939.

Trollope, Frances. *Paris and the Parisians in 1835*. 2 vols. London: R. Bentley, 1836.

Trollope, Frances Eleanor. *A Memoir of Frances Trollope*. 2 vols. London: R. Bentley and Son, 1895.

Vivent, Jacques. *La Vie Privée de George Sand*. Paris: Hachette, 1949.

Wagenknecht, Edward. *Cavalcade of the English Novel*. New York: H. Holt and Co., 1943.

Whitridge, Arnold, ed. *Unpublished Letters of Matthew Arnold*. New Haven: Yale University Press, 1923.

Williams, Blanche Colton. *George Eliot*. New York: Macmillan Co., 1936.

Winwar, Frances. *The Life of the Heart: George Sand and Her Times*. New York: Harper and Brothers, 1945.

Wise, Thomas James, and Symington, John Alexander, eds. *The Shakespeare Head Bronte, The Life and Letters*. 4 vols. Oxford: Printed at the Shakespeare Head Press and published by B. Blackwell, 1932.

Woolf, Virginia. *The Common Reader*. Second series. London: Hogarth Press, 1932.

Index